Hope, Inspiration, and Wisdom

A Treasury of Thoughts on Coping with Kidney Disease

by
Renal Support Network

Hope, Inspiration & Wisdom:
A Treasury of Thoughts on Coping with Kidney Disease

ISBN 978-1482643534

Copyright © 2013 by Renal Support Network

Printed in the United States of America.

Contents

2011 Essays   173

What hobby helps improve your quality of life and helps you forget the many challenges kidney disease presents?

2012 Essays   217

What small act of kindness by a health care professional made a difference in your life?

Introduction

A Message from Lori Hartwell

One of the most important, illuminating, and beneficial things I've learned from overseeing the Renal Support Network's (RSN's) Annual Essay Contest is that there's a huge, untapped reservoir of literary talent among patients with renal disease. These essays provide an innovative, perceptive, and touching look beyond the mundane to the profound and spiritual that often elicits a grateful tear or a joyful laugh from the reader. They also provide much food for thought and illustrate the overwhelming challenges that chronically ill people face every day.

Since 2002, we have read well over a thousand essays. From the first, we knew that we'd struck a gold mine of literary talent. If, as is often said, we all have a book in us waiting to be born, then there should be a substantial library awaiting its grand opening among patients with kidney disease.

Clearly, there's a plethora of talent within the renal patient community. I believed that we needed to tap into those skills, to show society that patients who have undergone dialysis and kidney transplantation are a valuable resource that is too often underutilized.

Perhaps this highlights what the Medicare End-Stage Renal Disease Program was originally all about—not only supplying life-saving treatment, but also recognizing and bringing out the hidden talent so many of these patients have. They inspire their fellow patients. They realize instinctively that a chronic illness such as kidney disease is too demanding if they don't have hope.

We at RSN believe that these essays inspire and ignite hope. You can read the book from start to finish or you can dip into it at any point and find the people behind the essays—their hopes, their dreams, their courage, and their humanity. You'll laugh and cry with them. You'll feel that you know them.

Reflect and enjoy!

Chronically Yours,

Lori Hartwell

About Lori Hartwell
& Renal Support Network

Lori Hartwell is the Founder and President of the Renal Support Network (RSN), a nonprofit, patient-focused, patient-run organization that provides nonmedical services to those affected by chronic kidney disease.

Lori, who has had four kidney transplants and was on dialysis for almost 13 years, has emerged as a powerful example of how to lead a complete and productive life despite chronic illness. She created RSN to let her fellow patients know that they don't have to make this journey alone.

She's also an author in her own right. Her book "Chronically Happy: Joyful Living in Spite of Chronic Illness" describes her philosophy of life and her personal coping skills and has served as an inspiration to the many thousands of people who have read it, whether they have a chronic illness or not.

Mission

The Renal Support Network (RSN) is a nonprofit, patient focused, patient-run organization that provides nonmedical services to those affected by chronic kidney disease (CKD).

RSN strives to help patients develop their personal coping skills, special talents, and employability by educating and empowering them and their family members to take control of the course and management of the disease.

Learn more at www.RSNhope.org.

2002 Essay Theme

How the staff
at your dialysis unit
or transplant center
encourages you to
live a fulfilling life
in spite of kidney disease

I See; I Hear

Jim Burton

I SEE. I HEAR.

I take precious fluid from fragile humans.

I clean it,

Detox it,

Bless it, and send it back.

I improve their lives. For a time, I can help them.

I share my patients' life blood. I share their souls.

I know when they hurt,

When they smile,

When they want to die, and

When they want to live.

I want them to live. So do others.

I see Technician CG. A distressed Mr. Patient approaches her.

"My fluid is over. Way over. 7.1! I have no will power. This thirst is 24/7. None of the tricks and gimmicks work. I'm thirsty!" Mr. Patient sobs.

Maybe he thinks that, by crying, he'll get rid of some of the fluid. His tears make two tiny waterfalls. Technician CG takes Mr. Patient's hand.

I hear: "It's going to be all right. Let us take care of it. That's our job. We'll take off as much as we can. You just sit and relax."

She doesn't nag. She doesn't berate. She doesn't scold. She calms his boiling blood.

I see a large patient with creamy white hair stumble-walk to his chair. He's an ancient one. His offspring accompanies him. I can clean his blood, but, sadly, I can't help with his other condition. The offspring calls it "Oldtimers." I think my hearing is getting slushy. Nurse PX approaches the large creamy patient.

"How are you today?"

"I'm fine."

"Did you have a good Thanksgiving?"

"Yes."

"What did you have to eat?"

"Yes."

"Did you eat too much?"

"Yes."

"Were you a bad boy?"

"Yes."

Nurse PX inserts my connecting needles into the creamy arm with great care. It hurts. The large patient winces. He's frightened and confused. But there's a caring nurse-hand letting him know that the pain will pass. Someone cares.

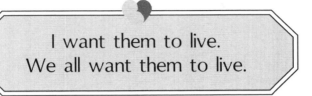

I want them to live.
We all want them to live.

The large patient's confused and frightened blood bounces around inside me. He feels comfort from somewhere, from someone. He says, "Yes."

I see Nutritionist RT. She's the human with the loud-colored sweaters. Her colors sometimes hurt my digitals. On one dialysis day, RT offers a patient the privilege of being a mentor—to help and support other patients who are having diet and/or fluid problems.

The patient accepts. His blood races through me with giggly excitement and warmth. I hear him tell young woman patient with deep dark hair, "There are three 'F' words to remember when you're a dialysis patient. Do you know what they are?"

She hesitates. "Uh, no."

He smiles. "Fluid, Phosphorous, and Fun!"

I think that was human humor. Interesting approach to healing—humor. Mentors and humor.

Our humans would improve on such a diet. My Patient J's

blood emits positive signals when Doctor M comes to visit. I know it's him because the overhead lights bounce off his partially balding top, creating a pinkish aura. I see them shake hands, and I hear them exchange greetings:

"You're looking good."

"Hi, Doc, how are you?"

They discuss Patient J's blood work and all of the other important numbers. And then Doctor M says, "I read your play as requested. Wonderful! You have a wonderful piece of work. What are you going to do with it? Any ideas for play number two?"

They chat. Just chat. And Doctor M sits. Yes, he sits! Most docs stand over their patients like a god. Doctor M meets his patients eye-to-eye and gives them some of his time. Dialysis patients don't know how much time they have left. That thought makes their blood heavy and makes my tubes sag. By chatting, Doctor M lets his patients know that he has time for them.

Doctor M hands Patient J a book. "It's a Nero Wolfe mystery. Interesting."

Patient J hands Doctor M a book. "Here's 'A Walk in the Woods.' Very funny. I didn't expect that. I loved it."

Before my digitals, I see a lending library and two book critics! They chat about Stephen King. Doctor M leaves.

Patient J doesn't need Ativan or any of those drugs right now. His blood is content.

I share their souls.

I know when they hurt,

When they smile,

When they want to die, and

When they want to live.

I want them to live. We all want them to live.

The Gifted People of Shoreline Dialysis

Paul Cervoni

"PAUL, HONEY, WAKE UP! Your treatment's over. Any plans for the weekend? Sightseeing? Country fairs? Auctions? Vermont?" my nurse asks as she checks my arm and records my weight.

"Yeah. We're off for an overnight in Vermont."

I leave the clinic to a chorus of "goodbyes" as one of the nurses yells, "Come back when you can stay longer!"

We all laugh.

As I sit in the reception area waiting for Transit to take me home, I gaze once again at the unit's pet bulletin board, our social worker's project displaying humorous photos of the cats, dogs, and horses that belong to patients and staff. As I sit there smiling, I hear laughter coming from the clinic. A nurse comes through the door wheeling a 90-year-old patient, helping him into his coat (it's 95 degrees outdoors) and laughing hysterically.

"Did you hear about Nurse Jody's kitten?" she chuckles. "Yesterday, the vet changed its name from Athena to Plato!"

More laughter all around.

Transit is late again. I close my eyes and start to reflect on my past 22 months at Shoreline Dialysis. What is it that makes me want to come here for daily dialysis? Why, during a recent long hospitalization, did I miss the clinic and its staff so much?

> "A cheerful heart is good medicine,
> but a downcast spirit dries up the bones."
> ~ Proverbs 17:22 ~

When I began at Shoreline, I'd just completed a 40-year academic career and found the prospect of being one of 12 patient designees for a dialysis-six-times-a-week-for-one-year study an exciting prospect. It would be like one of the many research programs of my school career, this time working with doctors, physician assistants, nurses, technicians, and researchers in New York and California, all to convince the U.S. government to fund daily dialysis because patients proved to be healthier in a program that could be more cost-effective.

Although the research was a key factor in my thriving in this clinic, I knew it was more than this alone that has brought me to my present optimal health, positive attitude, and zest for life. It was clear that I was in the care of a very select group of professionals especially chosen for this clinic. They were knowledgeable, devoted, compassionate, loving, and sometimes even eccentric. In addition to the "tell-all" blood tests, they could read every furrow in your brow.

I bump along on the ride home, 90-year-old Joseph in his wheelchair beside me, clutching a precious bag of fresh cherries for his wife. Our clinic secretary had purchased them for him on her lunch hour.

I feel content and think back to one of my first visits to Shoreline. That day, I'd tried to refuse treatment. This brought an immediately closed curtain and a gathering of staff. I felt I'd earned my misery and simply wanted to disappear. Thirty years of diabetes, a leg amputation, and end-stage renal disease were ample reasons to quit.

After some minutes of an implacable attitude, I was shocked as I heard the social worker say, "I'll make arrangements with hospice."

In a moment, the curtain still closed, I found myself alone with Nurse Jody. She stared directly into my eyes.

"Hey, you! Did it ever occur to you that you brighten our lives by just coming here every day? Do you know that people here go home and worry about you? Now, get your butt into that chair so I can put you on the machine!"

We both laughed. I'd never felt so loved.

From that day on, I realized that I was with a well-orchestrated, gifted staff capable of motivating a room of machine-dependent people into functioning, laughing, fulfilled human beings determined to live full lives.

The bus trip is over. I arrive home feeling a body and spirit healing at the hands of people who know how to treat patients with state-of-the-art medicine and with the healing touches of humor and laughter.

When I returned to the clinic Monday morning, I heard gales of laughter. One of the patients had complained that she couldn't see the clock, so the nurse took it off the wall and placed it in her lap.

I thought of something I'd read in the Old Testament: "A cheerful heart is good medicine, but a downcast spirit dries up the bones." (Proverbs 17:22)

One by one the staff came by and asked, "How was your weekend?"

"Wonderful," I replied. "I drove my car for the first time in two years!"

He Knows How It Feels

Saundra Davenport

THE STAFF AT MY DIALYSIS UNIT encourage me in many ways to live a fulfilling life in spite of kidney disease. Some ways are overt, and others aren't so obvious to someone who doesn't need a lift in spirit from time to time.

Although the staff perform their duties in a professional manner, each of them finds the time to answer any questions I have. If they don't know, they're willing to get the answer. They make me feel special by knowing my personality to the point that if I'm not my usual self, they ask me if something is wrong.

I know that all units aren't fortunate enough to have staff who have kidney disease or who have had a kidney transplant. However, my unit has a staff member who has experienced (medically) the same things I've experienced.

A lot can be said about his sensitivity toward the patient's plight. He knows first-hand what it's like to have treatments over the years and all the problems associated with those treatments. He knows how it feels to have two 18-gauge needles inserted in your arm at least three times a week; how it feels when your blood pressure drops time after time; how it feels to have to take medications that sometimes make you ill; how it feels to be unable to have all those delicious, tasty foods and drinks; and, finally, how it feels just to be able to go to the bathroom and urinate (a natural function that most people take for granted).

> He knows how it feels to have two 18-gauge needles inserted in your arm at least three times a week.

But beyond what we share as patients, this staff member alone inspires and encourages me to be all that I can be and do all that I can for myself. He's had three transplants over many years, yet he still works a long, 13-hour day. He never considered giving in to his disease and staying home to dwell on his ailments. He inspires me to live a fulfilling life in spite of kidney disease.

Next, I believe that the more a person is educated about a subject, the more equipped or prepared he or she is to fight the battle and win. The staff at my dialysis unit arm me with the knowledge I need to live a quality life. All I need to do is listen, learn, and adhere to the advice given to me by those who know how to prolong my life in spite of all the changes my body experiences.

I'm constantly reminded of my responsibility to be receptive to the things I have to do to have a good quality of life. And when I look at the whole picture, it's ultimately my responsibility to watch my diet, police my fluid intake, and engage in activities that stimulate me physically, mentally, and emotionally.

Aside from this one staff member who especially motivates me, the other staff motivate me in ways that I'm sure they're unaware of. Their attitudes, work ethic, knowledge, and enthusiasm are quite noticeable. Even their bright, colorful clothing is an encouragement.

When I have to give up three (sometimes four) days of my life just to stay alive, it's important to me to be in pleasant, neat, and bright surroundings. My unit is kept clean by the staff, and that goes a long way toward promoting a sense of well-being and of being well taken care of. The staff support us emotionally by taking us aside and comforting us when we have personal problems. They support us socially by holding bake sales to raise money to give us a Christmas party (complete with gifts), and they keep us entertained by playing games with us while we receive our treatments (they serve us and entertain at the Christmas party, too). Now, that's fun!

Leading a fulfilled life while having end-stage renal disease merely means accepting my lot in life and handling it with all the zeal I can muster and making those around me feel comfortable enough to treat me with loving care and, most important, with respect.

I end by saying that each (and I mean each) staff member has affected my life and encouraged me to do all that I can for myself and for others. And doing things for others has allowed my life to soar to heights that are hard for me to explain. I just feel joy.

I'm happy and so very grateful to have my dialysis unit!

A Brighter Day

George Holwick

WHEN I WAS YOUNGER, all I wanted was to live a normal life. To live a life without medicine, monthly hospital visits, and surgeries to save my life. I hated the fact that "normal" people looked at me as an outcast.

Some people would say that I was too different and that I could never be like them. Others tried to give me a different point of view, a view that was as golden as a sunrise. These people are special. They showed me that I should laugh. The negative people laugh because I'm different, but I laugh because they're all the same.

When I was younger, I had a kidney transplant. My life changed drastically. From then on I would have to take medicine for the rest of my life. I would have scars that I could do nothing about. This wasn't my choice; I didn't want to live like this. I wanted to go out and play, to be free from the worry of losing a vital organ more easily than anybody else.

The staff at Children's Mercy Hospital taught me that if I

looked on the brighter side of my condition, then maybe I would realize that I was stronger than the normal people, that I've been through so much more than they have, that I've played doorbell ditch with Death. But instead of running away, I laughed in his face. He (Death) didn't and never will have power over me, and neither does anybody else. These great people showed me that.

They're the light in the darkness. They're regular people, but they give you the impression that they could take on the world and

> ...I've played doorbell ditch with Death.
> But instead of running away,
> I laughed in his face.

they give you the courage to join them—to walk on the moon or go to the depths of the ocean. They try to make your life just a little brighter, anywhere, at any time. Large or small, they care about everyone. They cared for me, and they actually listened to me.

The staff at Children's Mercy Hospital didn't just show me how to face up to those who couldn't understand or just wouldn't understand. They're the ones who saved my life. They're the ones who performed the surgeries and stuck foot-long needles in me. And it's not just the surgeons. It goes down to the janitors, who make sure that your room is bacteria free so you don't get any sicker than you already are. It's like one big family, and I was a guest whom they seemed to want to treat with the greatest respect. And now I respect them.

So, if we're all going to take one role in life, to take a role that can be highly respected and get you more friends than you can think of, then maybe you should become part of the Children's Mercy family. And if you ever see me, George Holwick, there, I'd love to meet you because I feel that, if you're a member of the Children's Mercy family, then I've known you my whole life.

2003 Essay Theme

Kidney disease:
Redefining what is
important in life

The Real Miracle of Family

Ninette Haro

IF YOU'D TOLD ME only a dozen or so years ago that I'd need a kidney transplant or dialysis to survive, I wouldn't have known what you were talking about. Literally. Before May 1995, I'd never given a first, let alone a second, thought to my kidneys.

When I was told that I had kidney failure, I was living on my own for the first time and immediately came home to tell my mom. I was devastated. If it hadn't been for my mom and my brother, David, I have no idea how I could have accomplished the monumental task that lay ahead, both surviving with kidney disease and going through all of the treatments necessary to stay alive. In fact, if it hadn't been for both of them, I very well might not be here to write this at all.

In a flash, my life as a relatively carefree 23-year-old was over. I could no longer afford to waste energy, be it on rotten boyfriends, flaky friends, or whatever appeal nightclubbing held for me back then. I needed reinforcements.

I needed my family.

On Sunday night, January 31, 1999, my mom and my brother walked beside me as I was wheeled to the operating room to get my new kidney. My mom knew I was scared. She leaned in close to my ear and said gently, "You'll be all right. We're survivors!"

By 1:30 a.m., my 2-year, 3-month wait on peritoneal dialysis was over. My pre-owned kidney was pumping urine out as efficiently as if it had been my very own healthy native kidney.

I came to very shortly in that recovery room and, when I did, I felt like I was a cotton ball, warm and fuzzy. Sounds were muted, and I remember someone asking whether I was in pain. Pain? It was only a faint, far-away sensation, and I drifted back into my cocoon before I could answer the nurse.

My family was there in the dawn hours as I came to in my hospital room. Mom and David said I was smiling a lot and doing something I've never really done before in my life. I was doped up and giving the thumbs-up sign. To this day, I'm eternally grateful that a video camera was nowhere in sight.

I called my mom from Stanford two days post–kidney transplant. I was weeping and felt emotionally naked, as if all of my defenses had been stripped off, leaving my psyche raw.

"Mom, I don't feel like I deserve this transplant," I said, even though I'd been on the waiting list for over two years.

"Of course you do! Don't think like that. You've been given a wonderful chance."

My emotions were paying for having 100 milligrams of prednisone coursing through my veins at 100 mph. My mom stayed on the phone with me for over two hours until I calmed down and fell back to sleep.

Kidney disease taught me that time is finite and to keep only the most important things close to your heart. Don't clog your life up with meaningless concerns, the ones that creep into your life and shift your priorities and perspectives so that you no longer take time with the people you cherish most. Looking back now at the sacrifices, support, love, and caring my family gave me willingly and unconditionally, I know now the real miracle of family that had existed long before my battle with kidney disease began.

> Kidney disease taught me that time is finite and to keep only the most important things close to your heart.

As I write this, life as I knew it has been transformed again. After having battled a chronic illness that became terminal, my brother passed away in January 2002, and seven months later my mom joined her son in heaven.

Although I grieve profoundly and will mourn their passing for the rest of my life, I know that I've been truly blessed and that my life is all the better for having had them in it. Blessed with good health, I was able to serve as a caretaker for both my mom and my brother, as they had for me. I now have an empathy that comes only from the first-hand knowledge of living with a chronic disease. I know now that I'm truly a survivor, just as my mom had told me.

I can never repay them for all they did for me, but I will honor their lives by making the most of the life I have now—one prednisone-filled day at a time.

The Ultimate Adventure is the Infinite Day

Lori Vivian

As I sit here and stare at a blank computer screen, I try to find the words that define my life now. I remember when I first became sick and the doctor told me that I had kidney failure; I went home stunned, scared, and resigned. My friend is a registered nurse, and I looked up end-stage renal disease in one of her medical books.

I wanted to know exactly what I was facing. No secrets for me. I wanted to know exactly what the facts were. I'm a fact person, a person who believes that information shall always set you free. The big official book of medical facts informed me that patients with kidney failure are defined as "marginal." They're people with a terminal disease, people who can be maintained for an indefinable amount of time with dialysis or transplantation. But there's no cure, only treatment. Hence the term "marginal," neither here nor there, but defined as somewhere in between.

I thought: "No way. I'm many things, but never marginal. I either jump with both feet, or I don't jump at all. I'm not a fence sitter.

I'll go forth and conquer. I'll be true to my nature. All I need is a plan."

And therein lies the problem: try as I might, no plan was forthcoming. I investigated, questioned, researched, and still came up empty. I started dialysis three days a week, four hours a visit; made friends with the other "marginal" people; learned the lingo; measured

> Today will be what's important.
> Tomorrow doesn't own me any more.
> Today is infinite.

my life by liters of intake; rode the exercise bike like a hamster on a trip to nowhere; learned to get used to needles stuck in my arm like something from a bad late-night-movie experiment; and still no plan. One year turned into two years, and here I sit trying to define the difference in my life now.

I suppose the fact that I have no plan is a major difference. Learning to live a life without a plan, without a safety net, without a direction, without an idea of what tomorrow will be or what I plan to do has turned out to be the ultimate adventure.

Before my illness, I plotted and planned, set out to complete my goal, and, if all else failed, sheer force of will would see me through. Because I had a plan, everything was all mapped out, with any and all escape routes marked in case of an emergency—not to mention the several backup plans just for good measure. I was the person who actually listened to the flight attendant when she pointed out the exits, read the fire escape routes that are posted on the back of hotel doors, made lists, and always made sure the "just in cases" were covered.

Now I live every day without the Big Plan. I wake up and face today, and that's the plan I live by. At first, I found it overwhelming. How does one get through the day this way? Chaos would rule, I was sure of it. Yet somehow, while I was walking on this undefined path that's now my life, I've found peace. Living each day as it comes, accepting what I cannot change, no longer tilting at each and every windmill that crosses my path, and taking the time to see what's here and now has taken the place of the plans and lists for all the tomorrows. Chaos didn't take over.

As a matter of fact, instead, there's a freedom I didn't expect—the freedom to make mistakes, the freedom to be imperfect. And instead of finding that my time is less, I've found that my time is more. I have more time to watch the world and the people around me. I have the time to read the books I'd always planned to read someday, I have the time to say the things I always meant to say, I have the time to hold all that's dear to me, I have the time to be surprised by the now, by the just this minute.

Today will be what's important. Tomorrow doesn't own me any more. The people in my life, the love I have for them and they have for me, is enough now because it's what I have today that I can cherish, and today is not marginal.

Today is infinite.

The Broken Wing

Athena Bozakis

I WAS FLYING HIGH! In spite of a humble beginning, an abusive marriage that ended in divorce, and three children to rear, doors had opened for me, and opportunity seemed to have chosen me for its one true mission. My career in computer technology was in full swing. I'd mastered the logic and risen in stature.

The children had grown up and started new lives. This was my time to amass retirement funds and plan for a future full of European tours and artistic fulfillment. Maybe I could even rekindle my social life after years of heavy responsibilities.

My thoughts that morning in August 1989 were on an upcoming computer conference in Boston. I'd showered and then used the toilet once more before I dressed. When I turned to flush it, my hair stood on end. The water was filled with blood!

I think I went into total denial at once. I know that I was shaking as I made my way to the bedroom. Then I continued to get dressed and numbly drove to the office. I didn't go near a bathroom again until about 2:30 that afternoon. There it was again! This was when I decided that I'd better see a doctor.

My family doctor was perplexed by the results of the blood work. He sent me to an internist, who gave me a jug to fill with urine over the Labor Day weekend. I returned the filled jug on Tuesday morning and went to work, even though I was so bloated that my clothing hardly fit. It was difficult to walk and even more difficult to breathe.

Did that stop me? No way. My projects were waiting, and there would be phone messages to return. You see, I was a dedicated professional with a very important position.

The receptionist handed me a message as I emerged from the weekly staff meeting. She said I was to call this doctor back immediately. The name was a new one.

I made the call. He explained that he was a nephrologist and that I was in serious trouble. Maybe he could save me. Maybe? What?! Sitting at my desk, I felt rather detached from the whole scenario. I should come right to the hospital. Don't stop at home. Call my family and my priest. What? As I hung up, I told the director that some sensationalistic doctor needed to be assuaged. We decided that I would go and take care of whatever it was and return to work for the afternoon.

That day started a journey down the twisted path of end-stage renal disease. I went through experimental treatments, surgery, depression, bone disease, changes in diet and fluid intake, and lifestyle modifications. My valiant efforts at trying to continue working until retirement age failed. Seven years of struggling with full-time employment and evening dialysis finally took their toll, and I retired on disability at age 55.

> It was only after my wing was broken that I was able to refocus on the real meaning of life.

Depression, isolation, and hopelessness were my constant companions for the first months. Even the old three-story homestead had become an albatross. It took me a year to relocate, buy a new computer, and notice that the sun rose every day. A lot of the credit goes to my family and friends. There was always somebody there to pick up the pieces.

My reawakening started with a church dinner that needed volunteers. Then it was a plea from the literacy council for people to mentor illiterate adults. Later, I heard about GED classes begging for a teacher. And there was always a need at the clinic to raise the spirits of my fellow patients who sat strapped to the machines three days a week.

Friends and family gained a new, accessible resource for problem solving. As I got more and more involved, it occurred to me that if I were still working, I couldn't have participated in these vital tasks. I wouldn't have been there to fill in the gaps. My

God-given talents would still be tied up building personal wealth. It was only after my wing was broken that I was able to refocus on the real meaning of life. I could use my talents to inspire hope, expand the horizons of my fellow man, and help others regain their dignity and dream of possibilities.

Wow! What a chance to prove myself worthy of extended life on this planet!

I rejoice that when disaster struck, it chose a way to keep me grounded but alive and capable of rising above my personal paradigm with grace.

2004 Essay Theme

Tough times:
A memory or dream
that gets me through

A Memory of Butterflies

Luz Mazano

AFTER 12 YEARS of living dialysis-free, I faced transplant failure. It was difficult to accept, for I knew very well the life that awaited me. I would once again have to go through hemodialysis week after week, month after month, and year after year. I struggled through feelings of anger, hopelessness, and finally acceptance. I thank family and friends for being there, for holding my hand and wiping away the tears...

But most of all, I'd like to thank a butterfly.

I clearly remember the day. It was warm. The sun was shining brightly, and I was kneeling in my garden pruning the Shasta daisies. My heart was heavy, and my soul felt like it could never be mended. How could I face going back on dialysis, being tied to a machine again, week after week, and month after month?

As I tended to the flowers, a butterfly came fluttering around near the daisies. I was surprised, for she came so close and began dancing around me. Every so often, she would land on my hand.

> No matter how winding the road,
> within us are the strength
> and the courage to carry on.

As I watched her, I noticed that, although she had a broken wing, she danced as if she were perfect. She played with me for a while and then, just as suddenly she came, she flew away. I cried there in the sun, for she reminded me of myself, a soul with broken wings.

She came to visit me that afternoon to say, "Fly in spite of your imperfections, dance in spite of your limitations, for life is beautiful and worth dancing to." An important lesson, God's message sent to me on butterfly wings, a reminder that life goes on, that the sun still shines, and that, after the storm, there are still rainbows to be seen: that no matter how winding the road, within us are the strength and the courage to carry on.

Take Hold and Ride, Cowboy!

John W. Caskey III

I'M 36 YEARS OLD and I've had type 1 diabetes for 31 years. I started dialysis the week before Christmas 2003. Yet in all my life experiences—the good, the bad, and the terrible—I always remember the lesson that taught me it could always be worse and that, usually, it just seems that everyone has it better than I do.

The past few months, I've learned not to focus on myself, but to focus instead on family and friends, and to love, learn, and be responsible with my health not only for myself, but for others as well. As I sit in our dialysis center and watch the nurses go back and forth between patients, I feel the need to thank them all for the caring and professionalism they share with each one of us. As I sit there, I'm able to remember my funniest and hardest time as a teen.

It was a hot summer night. I was 13 years old and thought I was unconquerable. I'd just participated in the Frontier's Day parade in a small town called Cache, in Oklahoma. I'd been to other rodeos, but tonight's was different. I was about to compete for the first time, and I was pumped!

I had my horse groomed and gleaming. He was ready for our grand entrance. I had my chaps on, my spurs clanging on the heels, and I can't ever forget my Stetson—it was practically glued to my head.

The time came, and we made our grand entrance. We followed the American flag around the pivots like everyone else. It felt like the only difference was that my horse and I were the only ones in the arena. It was as if everyone's eyes were on me.

The lights were bright and shiny. The crowd was screaming and hollering cheers at us. It's an indescribable feeling. The rodeo started, and with each event, I became tenser and more excited.

My event was coming up quickly. My dad sensed my tension and continually tried to calm me down so I would stay focused. After all, it was the most dangerous event for a cowboy. That's right—I was going to ride a bull!

When the announcer called my number, I was ready. I had my rope resined up, and I had my dad coaching me, encouraging me every step of the way, telling me that I could do it, that all I had to do was put my mind, heart, and soul into it and I could accomplish anything. He was right! He gave me support and unconditional love. He gave me discipline and honor. He taught me to be strong during my weakest times in life.

I got on that bull and made the 8 seconds. I received a score of 69. I stepped up on the chutes and cocked my head as my dad looked at me, and I almost cried out loud when I heard him say, "I'm proud of you, son! You did great!"

Of course, in my haste and excitement, I didn't realize that the score wasn't counted because I'd just ridden someone else's bull. My dad said not to worry: "You did it once. You can do it again." And I intended to! So I climbed on, and as I slid down on that bull, I caught a glimpse of the horns and the bulging back muscle. I could feel his breath blowing in and out.

> I was 13 years old and thought I was unconquerable.

Fear overcame me, and for the first time that night, I was terribly scared. I heard the announcer tell me: "Take hold and ride, cowboy! Take hold and go with him!" So I took my rigging and wrapped it in my hand, threw up my free hand, and shook my head.

As the gate flew open, the bull pounced and came down with thunder on his front feet, then spun violently! As he did, I fell into the center, which is the most dangerous place for a cowboy to be. I ended up eating hoof for supper and horns for dessert. I ended up semi-paralyzed for a month with a compressed vertebra, as well as a couple of broken bones and a lot of bruising. But still today, if given half a chance, I would ride again.

As I sit in the chair and listen to the swishing of blood being dialyzed and see it flowing through all the tubes, I return to times like that and remind myself: "It could be worse." In fact, there are times when I recline the chair and imagine the announcer telling me to "take hold and ride, cowboy! Take hold and go with him!"

But at the end of this ride, I stand up and walk away tall, clean, and fresh, and ready to take on another day. And as I call out my dry weight at the end, 94.5, I imagine it to be the winning score for my ride.

The Dream that Gets Me Through

Paul D. Rauch

I DIED LAST NIGHT.

The last thing I remember was looking at the clock. It was 11:32. When I opened my eyes, I was standing before a set of massive white gates. I reached out to touch them, and I heard a voice call my name.

"Paul, what are you doing here?"

I turned around to see a man in long white robes standing beside a huge book that was lying open on a carved white pedestal.

"I think I died," I answered. "Is this Heaven?"

"Yes. Heaven is on the other side of these gates. However, the question remains: Why are you here? It's not time for you to die."

"I'm so tired of being sick," I said. "I've been on dialysis for so long that I think it would be easier if I just gave up. Can I go in now?"

"You could," he said, "but before you do, you should know there's no turning back once you enter."

"That's fine with me. Let's get going."

"All right," he said. "Are you ready to turn your back on all those people still alive who are counting on you?"

"What are you talking about?" I asked. "I've been a sick man. How can somebody as sick as I was be of any use to anyone?"

> I've been on dialysis for so long that I think it would be easier if I just gave up.

"What about your wife? She relies on your knowledge and strength of will to make the daily decisions that are required to keep the family on an even keel. If she didn't have your sense of humor to brighten the dark spots that come into her life, she'd be living a miserable life.

"Your brother is constantly amazed by the things you write. He feels that you're the only real family he can look up to. He'll be lost without you there to see and talk to every day."

"Surely they could get along without me," I said.

"Perhaps they could, but what about Don?"

"What do you mean?" I asked.

"Early this year he lost his wife. He would have given up if it hadn't been for you. He made the statement that he would quit coming to dialysis except that he wanted to see what you were going to write next. You're helping to keep him alive.

"Another thing. Our Heavenly Father has given you the gift of writing, and you haven't finished all of the poetry and stories and songs He has for you to write and share with this world. God isn't finished with you yet. Now, are you sure you want to give up?"

I bowed my head in silence. Then, with tears in my eyes, I said, "No."

The great white gates began to fade and grow dim. I closed my eyes for a moment and when I opened them again, the clock read 5:30. Time to get up and go to dialysis.

2005 Essay Theme

That special someone

That Special Someone: My Daughter

Latrice Bolling

NEVER HAS THERE BEEN a dull moment in my life since she arrived.

Never have I known such a beautiful spirit.

Never have I been so impressed with the courage of one person.

Never did I expect to be so blessed in life.

Never did I expect her to bring such fulfillment and enrichment to my life.

Never have I been so inspired to be the best person I could be.

Never did I ever expect to hold the proud title of mother.

Never will I be able to repay my beloved daughter for changing my outlook on life.

Never did I expect that special someone to be born on my birthday and to say the most amazing words to encourage me.

From the time my daughter was born, I've been chronically ill. I'm a single mother. At 29 years old, I haven't known a single day in the past 11 years or so when there wasn't an ache or a pill to take.

I've suffered from lupus all of my adult life, and for the past two years, I've been on either hemodialysis or peritoneal dialysis.

My daughter learned early to adjust to lengthy hospital stays, surgeries, my fatigue at times, and unemployment. Even when I get down on myself, I look up, and there she is, smiling and still loving me for who I am and not what I am.

One afternoon, I was carelessly changing out of my blouse. I had a tank top on that exposed the catheter in my chest. I'd been on hemodialysis a little over six months, and I was ashamed to allow anyone to see my catheter. At times, I even felt like less of a woman.

I forgot that my daughter was in the room, and before I could cover my catheter, she said, "Mommy, what's that tube in your chest?"

The most amazing thing was that this little girl had been braver and more compassionate than most adults. She didn't squint. She didn't look away. She just asked, "Mommy, does it hurt?"

This began our open dialogue about dialysis. I explained that Mommy receives dialysis through this tube, and it doesn't hurt. Earlier, I said that my special someone said the most amazing words to me. She then said, "Mommy, it's okay. You're still pretty even if you have that tube in your chest. Mommy, I want to be just like you when I grow up!"

She took my breath away. I said, "Like me? What's so special about Mommy?"

I was thinking: "I'm chronically ill. Every time I think I have a leg up, there's another hurdle to jump. Some days, I feel like I'm

90. I feel that lupus has slowed many of my life's plans, and now here comes kidney failure."

Again, I asked, "Why do you want to be like Mommy?" This time my special someone answered, "Because you're smart, Mommy, and you're pretty."

> Even when I get down on myself, I look up, and there she is, smiling and still loving me for who I am and not what I am.

People are always revering me for my strength and ability to stand up for myself. What these people don't see is the human side of me. The side that gets angry when the peritoneal fluid goes into my abdomen and my belly expands. The vain side. The female side. The young woman who still wants to be active. The young woman who, on some days, says, "Here we go again!"

It's on these days that I look down at those beautiful brown eyes, and when she smiles, I know that I'm truly blessed. I know that she's my reason for achieving. When I think of how she loves me unconditionally and believes in me, I feel like I can fly.

My special someone inspires me to dream.

My special someone teaches me to love unconditionally.

My special someone has inspired me to continue with my

education. I went back to school to pursue a second bachelor's degree in public policy and obtained it. I plan to pursue a legal education and possibly one day participate in politics.

My next step is to start a nonprofit organization for patients with lupus. Finally, the biggest dream I have is to leave my daughter a legacy, not of fortune, but of perseverance.

My special someone has taught me that even in bad situations, if you have hope, you have a chance. Don't ever stop dreaming. Keep dreaming, and keep looking forward to something. And most important: never be idle.

A Friend Named Maggie

Jim Dineen

THERE SHE WAS AGAIN—just as she was every morning after my treatment. Each time I went through this, her eyes told me that she understood what I was feeling, and I could tell that she was sad. But most of all, she stayed with me as I removed my needles, serviced my equipment, and oh, so slowly walked downstairs. By the time we reached the bottom of the stairs, we were talking, and she knew that I felt okay again.

When the really hard times hit us in life, a friend can be the only thing standing between us and insanity. I was diagnosed with kidney disease in June 1998 and met Maggie in October of that year. I believe that God brings relationships into our lives when we need them the most.

My disease not only hit me fast, it hit me hard. Going from no symptoms to a 40-pound weight gain in less than a month, from lifting weights every day to barely being able to walk, also in less than a month, was quite traumatic. I went from running a successful business to having no business at all in less than six months.

Maggie listened to me cry and scream and have all of the reactions of a person in shock. She did so with patience and understanding and with that "I'm here for you" look always on her face. As our friendship grew, I realized how much I needed her to be with me—to listen to me and just give me that last kiss and that understanding hug at the end of each day.

> When the really hard times hit us in life, a friend can be the only thing standing between us and insanity.

As my disease progressed, our bond grew stronger. And even though my illness worsened and my body began to show rather dramatic changes, all of which were negative, Maggie never let on that she knew.

Friends can sense when we need them, and they know that just being around us can really help the healing process. Maggie was such a friend. We'd have breakfast together and then attempt a short walk. Lunch wasn't much, as exhaustion would begin to set in around 12:30 or 1:00, so we'd just sit together and talk. She often made more sense of what I was saying than I did, but it was conversation nevertheless.

I had ten surgeries over the course of four years, and she was with me every time. She'd soothe my pain when I got home from each surgery and talk to me, in her own way, about my healing. I could look into her eyes and know that everything would be fine. With her by my side each day, I decided early on that I was going to beat this kidney disease and get back to a normal life. Even when one of my doctors told me that he'd never had a patient as sick as I was live for more than two years, I told Maggie that you can't believe everything you hear, and naturally she agreed. We were a team by then, and we knew that we'd win this one.

After 4½ years of some of the worst times I've ever experienced in my life, I convinced the transplant team that I could handle a transplant. During the course of my illness, I'd contracted liver disease as well, so convincing the doctors was no easy task. My entire family, including Maggie, cussed and discussed the possible outcomes, and then we agreed to go for it.

On November 11, 2003, I received a life-saving kidney from my loving wife. I've never looked back and am doing wonderfully today. Maggie and I still talk about those bad times, but we feel and show our happiness more often now.

My life is getting back on track again. Although we'll be paying the bills for a long, long time, I can now earn the income to pay them.

It's been a long and difficult journey. My family and friends have all shared in my survival and healing: my wonderful wife, my daughters and sons-in-law, my three grandsons (all of whom were born during the course of my illness), and, of course, Maggie—my beautiful and loving friend, my companion through good times and bad, my confidant and partner, my soft and cuddly buddy.

We'll always be special to each other. After all, we've been through a lot together. Friends—and dogs—are like that.

Sings in My Heart

Christine Sanders

THE PROFESSOR'S VOICE was clear and crisp as he read our names. Frantically, I searched the crowd again. She was out there somewhere, silently cheering me on as she'd done for eight years. I knew that my name would be next. I thought of our journey that had brought me to this moment.

Hello, I'm Christine Sanders. This is my story.

At age 16, I was angry and shy. I hated everyone because I felt different. I hated myself. My mother worked three jobs. My five older siblings were never home. So I pretty much stayed at home—cooking, cleaning, and reading books.

My only friend was the library. There I would read and reread books about college kids, successful kids, accepted kids... everything I thought I couldn't be.

I also worked part-time, but we still had very little. Nightly, we searched the garbage cans behind supermarkets for food. Often we were locked out of our home or had no electricity or phone. We couldn't pay our bills.

I hated school. My peers picked on me because I was poor and looked the part. With no support system, I was ready to drop out.

Secretly, I had a bold and wild dream. I breathed my dream when I was awake or asleep. I wrapped my dream around me when despair slid into me. But over time, my dream began to die.

Then Stacey, a student teacher, changed my life forever. She was everything I wasn't: beautiful, smart, kind, and popular. For weeks I ignored her, turning in blank assignments. She returned them with smiley faces on them. I rarely spoke; she encouraged me. I glared at her; she smiled at me. Once, I stayed after school to complete a make-up test. I don't know why, but I said "yes" when she asked if she could help me.

Stacey immediately became my overall mentor. She spent endless hours with me as I studied. She encouraged me when I became frustrated. She held me as I cried, crying with me. I talked to her about problems at home and about how afraid I was there. I confided in Stacey, telling her my secret dream. She listened to me as if I were important, not insignificant.

Daily, Stacey reminded me of my potential, encouraging me to pursue my dream. Because of her, I began to believe in myself. She was my lone cheering section. My grades began to get better. I discovered a whole new world beyond my neighborhood. We went to plays, sporting events, museums, and restaurants. I gulped it all down, afraid that one day it would all end.

Life at home was getting worse. Then, Stacey moved to another city to teach. Several months later, she asked me to come live with her and her husband, Brett. With all of my possessions in one large black garbage bag, I stepped out of my past and into my future.

Living with Stacey and her husband was challenging. The community whispered about us, saying hurtful things. Stacey and her husband ignored the gossip and continued to love me unconditionally.

> With all of my possessions in one large black garbage bag, I stepped out of my past and into my future.

I became more social, developing friendships and participating in sports and other activities. As my grades improved, Stacey began talking to me about my secret dream: pursuing college!

In the fall of 1993, I began my college career. Then, the following year, I was diagnosed with focal segmental glomerulosclerosis. My blood wasn't being cleansed properly because the blood vessels in my kidneys had become scarred. Instead, blood and protein were leaking into my urine. I had renal failure.

The news was devastating! But there stood Stacey, advocating for me as I entered the world of tests, doctors, and surgeries.

"Christine Sanders!"

The professor's voice grabbed my attention. As my Bachelor of Social Work diploma was placed in my hand, my composure crumbled. Crying, I imagined Stacey's hand in mine as I held my dream, firm and alive.

"We did it," I whispered. But somewhere I heard her say, "You did it."

As a teenage African-American female, I lived with a young Caucasian woman and her new husband. Our friendship succeeded because of our unconditional love and respect for each other. People said that it couldn't work. Stacey and I proved them wrong.

Now I'm embarking on yet another new journey: dialysis. Stacey's voice, though 3,000 miles away, still sings in my heart, "You can do it!"

And I know I can.

2007 Essay Theme

Aspirations for the future:
What gives you hope?

Hope Moments

Sherai Onibasa

"There's hope.
It doesn't cost a thing to smile,
You don't have to pay to laugh,
You better thank God for that."

—India Arie

THE R&B ARTIST, India Arie, caught the essence of hope when she created those lyrics. It's the simple things in life that give me hope: smiles from infants, laughter, nature's beauty, dew in the morning, the sun shining brightly on a summer day, or the sound of the waves crashing against some rocks. You can't place a price on these things. They're precious, and the joy I experience from these things gives me hope because I can allow myself to bask in the moment and simply enjoy life. I like to explain this experience as an identified moment that lodges itself in the midst of a deep breath.

Think about it…inhale…exhale. It's that split second that

nestles between inhale and exhale that I call my "hope moment." Hope moments give me the energy I need to help me achieve the goals that I have in life despite my kidney disease.

The hope moment can be described as that moment of silence where there's nothing happening except you and your thoughts. It's that moment that temporarily suspends life and brings you an inner peace. It allows you to forget about your troubles, relax, and even think about what's going to come next. It represents potential. Specifically, it gives me permission to focus on tomorrow.

> ...if I don't look forward to tomorrow, then I won't have any hope for today.

Yes, in that split second....Think about it...inhale...exhale.... I believe it's the tomorrow factor within the hope moment that allows me to continue to participate in life rather than simply observe it. It's the participation in tomorrow that fuels my aspirations for the future. So, what does the future hold? I don't know, but I do know that if I don't look forward to tomorrow, then I won't have any hope for today.

Tomorrow represents opportunity. It's another chance to have a "do over." With tomorrow, I can make amends. With tomorrow, I can try it again. With tomorrow, maybe that laugh that I didn't get to have today will come. With tomorrow, the possibilities are endless, and just thinking about those possibilities in that hope moment gives me what I need to press on.

Go ahead…inhale…exhale…. Are you getting it yet?

I believe that my hope moments have a lengthening effect on my life because they allow me to be grateful for the things I have today. This is so important because, in spite of my circumstances and all that I go through, the simple truth is many people don't have hope moments because they don't get another tomorrow. So as long as I'm still around, I'll smile, laugh, observe the beauty of nature, and enjoy all of the hope moments that life has to give me!

As a dialysis patient, you can experience many not so good days. A day that's filled with lengthy doctor appointments, multiple needle sticks, and/or chronic pain can really put a damper on your mood. However, for me, that thought of "if I can just make it to tomorrow," gives me the little glimmer of hope that I often need to make it through the rest of the day. The idea of looking forward to something rather than focusing on the unpleasantness that I may be experiencing is what tomorrow is about.

So when the challenges are abundant in a day, I simply inhale…exhale…and enjoy that hope moment. Doesn't that feel better?

Celebrate the Day

Beverly Betts

I BELIEVE THAT HOPE is where you find it, begging to be re-newed. Hope regained is even more precious because you know the value of its loss. There's a certain relief that hope gives—a comfort in the knowledge that there's an end. I hope because I lost it once, and I know the dark place the world is without it.

I remember the day I lost hope. It was June 15, 2000. This day came after I'd gone to doctor after doctor for over 18 months. None of them could figure out what was wrong with me. Finally, someone did. It was such a relief to have someone validate my ill-ness, to confirm that it wasn't in my head or because of my weight, as one doctor had told me. My relief was short-lived. This doctor told me that I had systemic lupus erythematosus with nephrotic syndrome and that, because of it, my kidneys were failing.

After finding out what that meant, I asked what he could do to fix me. Much to my surprise, he told me that he couldn't fix me. He said that I'd need dialysis sometime in the next five years and would probably live another 20 years before the disease became terminal. While he said this in much the same detached tone as you would tell someone what time it was, I froze.

The person I used to be died in that instant. I functioned on autopilot, living from day to day for the next three years. During this time I was half-living. I didn't look forward to anything. Nothing excited me. Even food didn't taste the same. I never made plans. I just got through the day with the least amount of thought or effort.

Though I continued school and finished my BA in December 2000, the dreams of a grand future as a profiler were shattered. I had a plan that didn't include being sick, and I felt powerless to revise it. I pretended to be okay, coping with the illness, but I wasn't. While my body had gone on, my mind was still sitting on the doctor's table, with his voice saying "20 years" echoing in my ears. I'd wanted to tell him that wasn't enough time for my plan, but what could he do about that? Family and friends tried to be supportive, but they couldn't really understand. The grief I felt at what I'd termed to be the loss of the life I'd planned was inexplicable. So I just flipped on the autopilot and slapped on a smile rather than trying to explain it. That seemed easier somehow.

Days turned into weeks, weeks into months, and months into three years. In March 2003, following a bad flare-up, my kidneys failed. The doctor told me I needed to get dialysis. When he explained I'd have to have a tube in my neck, I went off. I refused further treatment and left the hospital.

I went home, and my son asked me, "Mommy, are you all better now?" When I looked into his eyes and saw the hope there, something inside me clicked back on. I knew then that I had to fight against this illness and win. I had to win for Ian, my little boy. I couldn't let the light in his eyes die.

From that moment forward, I had a renewed purpose. It was to live the life I'd been given—when life gives you lemons, make lemonade. I know it sounds like a cliché, but it's so true.

> I realize that I should enjoy the life I was given for the time that I have it instead of squandering it on regrets.

The first step was to regain control. I'd been letting others make decisions for me because I simply didn't care any more. When I returned to the hospital, I questioned the doctor for the first time in three years, asking him about my options. I was empowered by the simple act of engaging in my own care. I didn't feel powerless any more.

The next step was to look outside myself. I had to let go of the past in order to conceive of a future. When I went to dialysis, I saw real sickness. This made me realize that things could be much worse. It also made me realize the needs of others.

I taught my son to read. Then I took him to a nursing home to volunteer with me as a reader for the residents. I got a sense of accomplishment greater than any I'd ever experienced. I was hooked. I became active in church again and joined several ministries. I volunteered for local politicians. I did anything to fill up those hours, days, and weeks that became my life.

Next, I started to set goals for the future. Before that, I felt that my future was gone, but now I know that my future is now. I realize that I should enjoy the life I was given for the time that I have it instead of squandering it on regrets.

I'm currently on the waiting list for a kidney and hoping to get it one day soon. Until then, I've started my own business where I work from home. Now I look forward to traveling and taking short trips. I plan to have a big blowout in Las Vegas for my 30th birthday in November.

Last, I celebrate the day. I cherish each day that I feel reasonably good, each occasion spent with my family and friends. I have parties every holiday, even the little ones like Cinco de Mayo or St. Patrick's Day. On the day after Thanksgiving, I cook again and call it Thanksgiving 2. I tell my family and friends that I love them each time I see them. I kiss my son awake each morning and put him to bed each night with a kiss.

A Man Named Mr. Black

Elizabeth Churilla

I STARTED HEMODIALYSIS on March 28, 1990. It was a very bad year for me. I lost my Dad to cancer, and I was getting progressively worse. I'd known for years that I had to go on "the machine," but I kept putting it off until I was so sick I couldn't walk.

I'd had my fistula made eight years earlier. So I was all ready to get started, but being scared was my biggest problem... But that day finally came. I was rushed to Presbyterian Hospital at the University of Pittsburgh Medical Center. I had to have treatments immediately, so they began.

I remember that the very first treatment was a nightmare for me because I'd waited too long to start. I was a very sick lady. I went through five treatments—one every day—until I lost all the poisons and fluid (30 pounds) that had built up in my body and made me so sick. I'd tell people never to wait until you're that sick because your treatments will be very hard on you. As soon as your doctor tells you it's time to start hemodialysis, do it!

My aspiration and inspiration came in the form of a man named Mr. Black—a little black man who took a liking to me. Why me? I'll never know, but I'm grateful for his wisdom. It was my last day getting treatments in the hospital. Then I'd start having my treatments in a clinic. I was lying sick in my bed when this gentleman told me to sit up. I managed to sit up and listen to his every word.

He started by telling me that he was 89 years old. He'd been on dialysis for over 20 years. He started to tell me things I never knew could and would happen to me. And I thank God he did. He talked to me for over an hour, and I listened to his every word.

> Every time I said, "I can't,"
> I heard him say, "Yes, you can!"

He told me I'd have sick days, when I'd just stay in bed, but I'd have good days and do all the things I needed and wanted to do. He told me I'd cry, but I'd also laugh. I'd be sad, but I'd also be happy. He told me I'd have treatments where I'd wish I were dead, but I'd have treatments where I'd be able to sing, dance, and laugh again. He told me that life sometimes throws us many misfortunes, but that God will be there to help make them more acceptable, and he was so right on everything he told me.

Mr. Black was my hero for a day. That next morning I was

going home. I wanted to see Mr. Black, my inspiration, but he'd died the night before. I was never able to say "thank you" or "goodbye."

But I learned so much from his wisdom. Why, that day, did I have my last treatment at that time? I'll never know the answer, but I needed to learn all he taught me in that little time. I learned how to manage my life while living on dialysis. From his words, I know that I can get sick and sad, but I can also get happy... and mad. Every time I said, "I can't," I heard him say, "Yes, you can!"

I became a dancer and did things I thought I couldn't and wouldn't ever be able to do. It's been 17 years now that I've been on dialysis, and, yes, I live by Mr. Black's words: "You can do it!"

I've had my bad times being on dialysis, but I've had my good times too. I'll be forever grateful for my friend in heaven, Mr. Black, my inspiration.

Thank you, my friend. Wherever you are, you saved my life in so many ways... I love you!

Hope Is Love

Margaret Sewell

WHAT GIVES ME HOPE is knowing that there's a God who's watching over me on a daily basis. To go even further, I'd say He watches over me on an hourly basis. Hope. Hope is who holds my hand.

I was diagnosed with chronic kidney disease (CKD) when I was just reaching my young adult peak. I'd been married a few years, and I had two small children. I was attending college on my way toward a BA degree in psychology. My passion was to help the deaf and hard-of-hearing community with social issues. I was doing my thing. Hope. Hope encourages me to soar.

Then suddenly my life changed. I needed emergency dialysis. Yes, a year earlier, I was told by my nephrologist, whom I respected, that eventually I'd have to go on dialysis. The mere idea of this happening to me never sank into my brain. I thought what he was telling me was never going to occur. When I was rushed from the doctor's office straight to the hospital, I knew then that I was in big trouble. Hope. Hope hid me.

Decisions needed to be made for the long term, and I had to be the one to make them. What method of dialysis should I choose, and which permanent access would best work for me? Hope. Hope held me up.

My nephrologist, Paul Crawford, MD, took such good care of me because he knew I was afraid. He walked me through this very strange situation that was going on within me. Hope. Hope saw me through.

After my first in-hospital treatment, per Dr. Crawford's orders, a television set with a VCR was wheeled into my room. The nurse handed me several videotapes explaining each type of dialysis and its delivery method. I began to view the tapes and educate myself about my illness. I wanted to learn as much as possible, as quickly as possible. I realized that I had to make some serious decisions without a lot of time to do it. Hope. Hope opened the door.

Dr. Crawford sat down and talked over my decisions with me. Since I had two small school-age children, peritoneal dialysis would be best. I agreed. Hope. Hope brings comfort.

The span of my life with CKD is 19 years and counting. I share the story about my first encounter with other patients everywhere I go. I believe we share the same experiences and can relate to one another. Hope. Hope is our connection.

It took me five years to accept what had happened to me. I was in denial. I just knew I'd wake up from this dream, and everything would be back to normal.

My children were a big help and support for me. My son, Antoine, would ask me every day when I'd return home from hemodialysis, "How was your day?" He was only 7 years old at that time. The sound of his voice when he said this brought comfort and joy to me. Chanel, my daughter, was 8 years old, and she thought I was saying my "kitties" weren't working any more. She would say, "Can we go get you another kitty?" Children are so precious at that age. They're 22 and 23 years old now, with children of their own. Hope. Hope is love.

> Hope is love...
> Hope is the future.

My marriage didn't survive my illness. We weren't strong enough as a couple to patiently wait for the good times to roll back around. A chronic illness can be stressful for the whole family. I was mainly concerned that my children were fine with my being ill. I didn't want them to go without the love and support of their mother. I was an active school parent before my diagnosis, and I didn't want that to stop.

I did peritoneal dialysis and hemodialysis until I received a successful transplant in January 2005. Instead of having dialysis treatments, I'm able to sleep in more, and I've gone back to college. Exercising is my new hobby because I have more energy. The same year I got my transplant, I became the grandmother of two handsome boys. Earlier in my illness, with my many ups and downs, I wouldn't have been here to see them. Hope. Hope is the future.

I encourage everyone diagnosed with any illness to get actively involved with his or her health care. The more you know, the better quality of life you can have. How well do you want to live? Ask questions. Search the Web. Talk to other patients, and keep an open mind. Your life is what you make it.

2008 Essay Theme

Funding a dream
for $100,000:
Giving back

Get a Mentor

Demmie Raysor

First, let me introduce myself. I was diagnosed with end-stage renal disease in the summer of 1999, and, typically for me, I went into denial. But that's never stopped me from doing what I do best: moving on. While the disease was taking control of my body, I began to read up on kidney disease. The more I read, the more I realized that I was going to be in for the fight of my life, a fight that—I'm here to tell you—I wasn't going to lose. But even now, when I look back on how far I've come, I realize that I have a ways to go.

Growing up in a family of ten with our father as the only breadwinner, we kids all knew how to dream, how to imagine, and how to improvise. Let me begin with my quest, or my adventure, about what I would do to inspire or to help fellow patients with kidney disease if I found a check in the amount of $100,000 in my mailbox.

First, I'd educate them. Once a person has been diagnosed

with renal disease and will need to begin dialysis, I'd have a fellow dialysis patient who has had the procedure—catheter, fistula, or graft—assigned to the new patient to share his or her personal story about the surgical process, the healing period, and what the incision will look like once it's healed. Although my brain knows this procedure will not only save my life but will also give me a better quality of life, as a woman, my heart tells me that I'll have a scar that will be unattractive and might limit my wearing certain clothing. To some this might seem superficial, but to a female, especially a young female, it's a very real concern. It's important to have affirmation from someone who's already been where I still have to go.

Once the patient has chosen a dialysis center, I'd have the manager of that center or his designee contact the patient to set up a personal tour. During the tour, the manager can explain to the patient what to expect and assign a mentor.

The mentor will share his or her personal story, answer any questions, invite the new patient to visit with other patients while they're being dialyzed, and talk about food choices. Mentors can also help prepare people for the emotional experiences they're going to go through that are common in all illnesses. We all do a balancing act between regulating our blood pressure, fluid gain, and high potassium and phosphorous levels. While dieticians and the medical staff will counsel patients and give them all the information they need to add years to their life, a mentor will give them what they need to add life to their years.

Alcoholics Anonymous (AA) has built a very successful treatment program based on the idea of ensuring that each new person has a mentor. There are things that we'll share on a one-to-one basis with a person who has walked or is walking in our shoes that we won't share in large groups or even ask a medical professional about.

> ...a mentor will give them what they need to add life to their years.

At least monthly, have people who are on dialysis and working share their stories. Or have transplant recipients come in and share their stories. Sometimes a person who starts dialysis isn't interested in a transplant, but as time goes on becomes more amenable to the idea.

Hosea 4:6 states: "My people perish for lack of knowledge." Let's not perish, let's educate! My desire is that all of my fellow patients be proactive about their health. Whether you've developed kidney disease because of life choices or genetics, it's important that you arm yourself with all the knowledge at your disposal.

Lobbying for Kidney Care

Kevin Reynolds

THERE IT IS. A check for $100,000, from out of nowhere, sitting in my mailbox.

Only one caveat: Do something good with it for other patients with kidney disease.

Oh, is that all? Really, I'd need 1,000 times that amount to make even a dent in accomplishing all that I would like… better centers, earlier kidney education, better physician awareness of end-stage renal disease (ESRD), and, of course, donors all around to fund these projects!

But as we patients all know, you do the best you can with what you have. So that's what I'll bear in mind with my hundred grand.

I'm going with the theory that you start at home—make changes in your own neighborhood, city, or county. Then, like a pebble dropped in a still pond, you wait for the ripples to spread the message. That's how I'm going to use these funds to try to move my state toward an opt-out program of organ donation. What's that, you ask? Well, instead of asking residents to sign a donor card on their driver's license saying that they opt in, they'd be asked to sign a card saying that they don't want to be a donor. This then begins the process of re-educating the populace to understand that they're considered an organ donor unless they say otherwise.

> Our old way of opting in for organ donation just isn't working.

While it sounds like a simple change, it's actually a complex process involving various state departments, rules and regulations, and, most important, the verbiage used on the actual driver's license.

Step one would be sponsoring a statewide meeting of all of the key stakeholders in this effort: transplant hospitals and doctors, health organizations, patient groups, the United Network for Organ Sharing, government agencies, and the state department of transportation. Information regarding the critical need for organ donors and the miniscule percentage of those who agree to be donors would be stressed, with an emphasis on the need for greater donor education. An action plan to change the current state policy would be created by the end of the meeting so that specific steps and assignments would be in place to begin the process of changing current regulations.

Part of the $100,000 would be used to contract with a knowledgeable lobbyist to assist with the effort in the state capital. Knowing the right legislators, their staffs, and government officials will be critical to pushing this movement along at a quicker-than-normal rate.

There's no doubt that this process will take time—nothing moves quickly in state government. However, while legislative wheels grind slowly, rallying public support can move more quickly. With an aggressive online and e-mail campaign and with the assistance of the stakeholder groups from the statewide meeting, a coordinated advocacy effort will begin to help influence our state leaders. Using the tag line, "Feel Great: You're a Donor," the campaign will be upbeat and positive, presenting this new concept as one that's not only easier but will also save thousands of lives a year.

Acknowledgment will be given to religious beliefs that don't embrace organ donation, but for the majority of residents, this opt-out idea will be shaped as the easiest way to provide life-saving organs to those of us who desperately need them. As this campaign gains speed, a coordinated outreach to state media outlets—television, radio, newspapers, etc.—will be undertaken to provide them with stories of local individuals waiting for donations and the simplicity of this new opt-out plan.

Our old way of opting in for organ donation just isn't working. Too many people are dying each day awaiting kidneys or lungs or hearts. The process that has been implemented is being presented in a backwards way, and often, in the crunch at the Department of Motor Vehicles, is probably being mentioned only briefly, if at all. Both a new kind of thinking and new philosophy about organ donation need to begin, and if they begin here, they could easily spread throughout the country.

I believe that this is the greatest long-range effort we can undertake to assist as many patients with ESRD as possible, now and in the future. Yes, we need new drugs and new technology, but we've got to find more donors to help keep us alive. That's why "opt-out" is my $100,000 effort.

The Portable Kidney

Mountrey Oliver

IF I FOUND A CHECK in my mailbox for $100,000 I would be very surprised and happy.

My first thoughts, after the initial shock, would be to make life easier for patients with kidney failure who are on dialysis. I would spend my $100,000 check on the research and development of a portable artificial kidney.

The portable artificial kidney, "Arty," would be similar to a pace maker. "Arty" would be to the kidney what the pace maker is to the heart. The artificial kidney would be a small machine about the size of a woman's fist. A patient would only need one artificial kidney that would be placed inside the patient's body through a small 2 inch incision in the area where one of the kidneys is located. The artificial kidney would consist of a soft pliable type material that has a lot of micro fibers similar to a natural kidney's nephrons. It would also take over the functions of a diseased kidney by filtering nitrogenous wastes and toxins from the blood and produce urine. The urine would then be stored in the urinary bladder until it is full. The urine would then exit the body through the urethra.

In addition to removing waste and toxins Arty would maintain the proper balance of water, electrolytes, and acids in body fluids. Arty would also help to regulate and lower high blood pressure. Patients that have Arty installed would no longer have to be concerned with their potassium, calcium and phosphorus levels. Patients would have more variety of food choices.

> "Arty" would be to the kidney what the pace maker is to the heart.

Unlike a transplanted kidney, anti-rejection drugs would not be needed for Arty since it is not made of living tissues and cells. If an infection occurs at the site where Arty is placed, antibiotics will be given. The only pills the patient will be required to take while using Arty will be hormone pills, vitamins and medications for preexistent conditions.

Arty would be powered by a tiny battery that will need charging every 5 years. To charge the battery a doctor or nurse would hold an electrical wand over the body where the artificial kidney's battery is located. The electrical charges from the wand would charge the artificial kidney's battery. Because Arty has a lot of micro fibers that act as filters which can get clogged or worn, Arty would need to be replaced every 10 years for optimum performance.

Arty would be another treatment option for patients with kidney failure. It would be moderately priced and insurance companies would cover the cost of the machine, surgery to install it and the cost of recharging the battery. Like the convenience of a kidney transplant, traveling will be easier for patients who have an Arty. This portable device will give kidney patients another chance at living a relatively uncomplicated and fulfilling life.

2009 Essay Theme

What helps me
live a joyful life
in spite of
kidney disease?

Strawberry

Ronda Matthews Cluff

PEMA CHODRON, an American Buddhist nun, tells the story of a woman being chased through the jungle by tigers. She comes to the edge of a cliff and, with the tigers behind her, has no choice but to climb down a vine. Once she does, she sees tigers below her too. What's more, a mouse is now gnawing at the vine to which she clings. What to do? She sees a ripe strawberry growing within reach, tosses it into her mouth, and "thoroughly" enjoys the treat.

When I read this story for the first time a couple of years ago, I was stunned. Yes, life is often a case of "tigers above, tigers below," as Chodron phrases it, but I couldn't wrap my mind around the idea of whole-heartedly, without a single reservation or concern, immersing myself in the joy of a small moment in the midst of a life-threatening challenge.

Over the days that followed, I began to own the strawberry story, because I have a potentially life-threatening challenge—polycystic kidney disease (PKD). I also have a "strawberry"—my

7-year-old daughter. She's a live-wire, and she's brought me into the world in a way that my introverted temperament never allowed. But because it's in my nature to dwell on my fear of the unknown and the things I can't control, I sometimes need to stop and ask myself out loud, "Where's the strawberry?" Most of the time, the answer is this 4-foot tall creature who doesn't take no for an answer and lives for small moments of joy. It's amazing how many joyful moments there are, and how powerful they can be, when you're really paying attention.

> It's amazing how many joyful moments there are, and how powerful they can be, when you're really paying attention.

I'm 42 years old and while my kidney function is pretty close to normal right now, I know it won't be that way forever. The impact of PKD on generations of my family has been enormous, and I've watched this disease take its toll on aunts, cousins, and my own mother. As I write, my mom has been on dialysis for 18 years, and a cousin is nearing the point of getting on a transplant list. Meanwhile, my own blood work and need for blood pressure medication show that PKD is staring me down, too. "Tigers above, tigers below."

But in every day there's at least one strawberry: an unexpected hug given so enthusiastically that I nearly lose my balance, sitting down as a family to watch The Wizard of Oz (for the 100th time), or going for a walk hand-in-hand on a late spring day (despite the salt-marsh mosquitoes).

I accept that life won't ever be without dilemmas and challenges and that sometimes things are not only messy, but downright ugly. I also know that if I welcome small, joyful moments into my life and live completely and without reservation while in them, I'll continue to be able to lead a joyful life.

For the Love of the Game

Marvin Burney

"HEY, BATTER, BATTER, SWING!" These are beautiful words to my ears.

I've been a hemodialysis patient for 14 years, but, more important, I've also been a volunteer coach in a youth baseball program for the past 24 years. My kidney failure and my years and years of dialysis have robbed me of some of the things that many 53-year-old men take for granted—like being able to work or being able to play 18 holes of golf on a hot summer day. But end-stage renal disease and dialysis haven't taken away my desire to be a volunteer in my community. Helping little kids learn to love the game of baseball is one of the greatest joys of my life.

At the youth baseball complex where I volunteer, I'm not a dialysis patient, I'm not a sick man, and I'm not disabled. There, I'm simply "Coach" to 15 precious 9- and 10-year-old kids. Yes, the players on my team know that I can't do everything that other coaches do. They see the scars on my arms from failed dialysis accesses, but it doesn't bother them. They touch the working fistula on my forearm and call it a "magic bumblebee" because it buzzes. They understand that I'm different, but it doesn't matter to them. In spite of everything else about me, my players know that I love the game of baseball and that I care about each and every one of them.

> At the youth baseball complex where I volunteer, I'm not a dialysis patient, I'm not a sick man, and I'm not disabled.

When I'm on the field with the kids, I don't have time to think about my health, my dialysis treatments, my doctors' appointments, my phosphorous level, or my physical limitations because there are more important things. Who's going to start on the mound today? Who's batting clean-up? Does every kid remember the signs for "bunt" and "steal"? Have we prepared our minds to be on top of our game? Did we give it our all? When the game's over, are there enough hot dogs for every child to have one (even if I can't eat one myself)? Does every kid have a ride home? Did everyone have a good time and learn something? These are the important questions on a youth baseball field.

Being a youth baseball coach in my little town, I have a clear purpose and I'm needed. I live in a rural, socioeconomically disadvantaged area of the country. Most of the kids on my team have been labeled "underprivileged," and many of them are being raised by single moms or, in some cases, grandmothers. Some of them come from families that are struggling just to keep food on the table, and a couple of them live in the government-subsidized housing project in town. Few of them have contact with a positive, adult male role model in their homes.

The kids on my team need me to teach them about sportsmanship—how to practice hard and then play hard, how to win with grace, and sometimes even how to lose with dignity. They need me to show them what it means to be part of a team; they need to see that raw talent and brute strength alone aren't enough and that, instead, determination and perseverance will carry them a lot farther. They need me to pat them on the back when they've done something good and to bench them when they get out of line. More than anything else they need me to be there at that field; they need to hear my laughter and see my smile. They need me to teach them "life's lessons," and if they learn something about the game of baseball, too, that's just the icing on the cake.

Dancing in the Rain

Jorita Lehman

I WAS BORN IN 1934 in the middle of the Great Depression. We had very little in the way of toys or things to play with. But we always had enough to eat, clothes to wear, and love in our house. I was the only child in the neighborhood in my age bracket, so I mostly entertained myself. I learned to watch the birds build their nests, delighted in a rainbow after I'd played in the rain, watched the sunsets, and went inside only when I was called by my full name.

I found joy in the smallest things, like climbing a big tree or crawling under the house to hide and drink an Orange Crush that I'd charged to my dad at the grocery store. I was also the neighborhood gossip. I went from door to door and repeated everything I heard the grownups say at my house and was rewarded with cookies and milk. So I can honestly say that I've been living a joyful life as far back as I can remember!

No one lives to be 75 without having experienced many

tragedies in life. I've had more than my share, but I refuse to let them get me down. I always have hope that tomorrow will be better, and it always is. When I start feeling depressed, I do something for somebody else. I call a friend, write a letter, or say something kind to those around me. I revert to my childhood and start finding joy in all the little things around me. I also call on my sense of humor to brighten my perspective.

> # Life isn't about waiting for the storm to pass...
> # It's about learning to dance in the rain!

When I learned that I'd have to go on dialysis, I was afraid. I couldn't imagine what my life would be like. My kidneys had been failing for nine years, but I thought that at my age, I would probably not live long enough for them to fail completely. But I was wrong. I was very ill and in and out of the hospital several times in the four months before I was placed on dialysis. My primary care physician was totally misinformed and told me that it would be terrible for me. But I didn't take his word for it. I got on my computer and started reading everything I could find about the machines. I also called a clinic and asked for permission to go and take a look at the facility and talk to the staff. They were extremely helpful and explained everything to me. One by one, my fears were alleviated.

The patients were sleeping peacefully or watching television.

I decided that I wouldn't let dialysis define me. I was the same person with the same capacity to find joy in my life. Dialysis was only a small part of my life, and so what if I had to be on that machine for the rest of my life!? Surely giving up a few hours a week to save my life and to feel better than I have in years wasn't too much to ask.

It's been almost two years since I started on dialysis. My health has improved greatly. I can drive my car now and travel (which is one of my great joys). I live a rich and joyful life. I have a wonderful family that's very supportive, and I've made so many new friends. I'm now a Patient Advocate for my clinic and hope to start a support group in the near future.

I have a little plaque in my office that pretty well sums up the way I prefer to live my life. It says, "Life isn't about waiting for the storm to pass... It's about learning to dance in the rain!"

2010 Essay Theme

Lessons learned from a book, movie, or song that help me deal with chronic kidney disease

"Life Is Like a Box of Chocolates"

Amanda Ratz

As a teenager, you think that terrible things happen only in the movies and would never happen to you. In our minds, we already have our life and our future planned out. But what happens when the wind blows something in your direction, something over which you have no control? At the age of 16, I learned that Tom Hanks's quote was so true: "Life is like a box of chocolates; you never know what you're gonna get."

I was diagnosed with an autoimmune disease.

A week after my diagnosis, I experienced my first admission into the hospital, followed by a kidney biopsy. My physicians entered my room and explained the bad news, stating, "Your disease is extremely active. We need to start an aggressive course of treatment immediately. We'll try everything possible, but there could be a chance your kidneys will fail and you'll need a transplant in order to survive."

Suddenly, my future was a huge question mark. My disease was attacking my joints and my blood vessels and causing excruciating pain. Mariah Carey's lyrics became my inspiration. Every day I listened to her sing "There Can Be Miracles, When You Believe."

I felt as if I was on a roller coaster ride, dangling off the back end, holding on for dear life by only my pinky finger. The disease was in charge, and there was nothing we could do to stop it. My faith was shattered, my hope seemed dim, and my courage was tested, but my strength kept me alive. Each day that song gave me the little bit of strength I needed to get through the next day.

> My faith was shattered, my hope seemed dim, and my courage was tested, but my strength kept me alive.

That year, I spent more nights in my hospital room than I did in my own bedroom. St. Louis Children's Hospital had become my home. But I never stopped believing, and my miracle finally arrived on December 11, 2000! A perfectly matched kidney and a second chance at life! My older brother, Matt, risked his life to save mine.

After the transplant, I made a promise to myself to better the lives of those affected by kidney disease and to increase the availability of all organs for transplantation. I know that paying it forward would help so many individuals and one day might even grant me my third chance at life. Becoming involved after transplantation was the wisest thing I've ever done. Sometimes helping those in need or cheering someone else up becomes the best medicine.

I'm no expert on living with a chronic disease, even after 11 years. Life is still like a box of chocolates, and each day I don't know what I'm going to get. I do struggle at times, and life isn't easy. I search every day to find that perfect balance where physically, emotionally, spiritually, and mentally I'll be at one. My goal is to find that perfect harmony! I try to remain positive every day. Over the years, I've learned that your attitude makes the difference in whether you sink or swim when dealing with an illness. If I wake up and feel like I don't have enough strength to continue, that's a bad day. I quickly remind myself of the gift of life I was given, keep my head held high, smile, and remember the promise I made to myself.

I'm a registered nurse, a sister, a friend, a daughter, a volunteer, and an advocate for chronic kidney disease (CKD). I am not my disease! This disease is just a part of me. It's the best, yet the worst, thing that's ever happened to me.

I've realized that the plans for our lives can be changed in an hour, a minute, or even a second. You can wake up one day, and your life could be changed forever. So what happens when the wind blows something in your direction that you can't control? Well, there isn't one thing that helps me survive CKD. Everything does! My family, friends, nurses, physicians, books, movies, and songs have taught me to "bend when the wind blows" and to pay it forward. They're also taught me that "there can be miracles, when you believe." Keep your head held high if the wind knocks you down. You weren't born to break, so pick yourself up, have faith, find your strength, and search for harmony. You're not your disease! Always remember to smile.

Swim

Kristi Flynn

I WAS 25, AND MY LIFE had just begun: I had a new job, a new house, and a new loving fiancé whom I was soon to wed. Everything was falling into place; I was finally an independent grownup! I had big plans and big dreams, and I just knew they were all going to come true—my whole life was ahead of me.

Then November 30, 2008, came along—a day I'll never forget. I'd been feeling under the weather for the previous few months. I thought it was just part of being a new teacher; it was no big deal. On that day, though, something was different. I was scared, and I didn't know why; everything felt urgent. I called my fiancé home from work to come sit with me until my mom could take me to the emergency room. I needed to feel better somehow; perhaps they could give me an antibiotic for this mysterious bug I'd picked up at school. I had no idea what was in store for me that day and for the future that had suddenly changed.

For the next week, life was a whirlwind. I found out that

my kidneys had failed and dialysis was imminent: words I never thought I'd hear. I thought I was invincible. How could this happen? What did I do to deserve this? Every day was filled with tears, and I couldn't stop them. I don't remember much from the hospital—blood tests, procedures, bad food—none of it sank in. I spent the next three months suffering through hemodialysis with a barely functioning catheter. That time in my life is a blur, a time I don't want to forget, but also a time I don't want to remember.

> "Swim for the music that saves you when you're not so sure you'll survive..."

I had one companion at the time—my iPod, where a song played continuously on repeat every session while I fought to sleep: "Swim" by Jack's Mannequin. "Swim" is a song about not giving up and continuing on with life, even if it keeps trying to drag you down. Even though my spirit was broken, there was no way I wasn't going to fight; I'm far too young to give up. When life didn't feel worth living any more and I wondered if I should stop trying, I'd remember the words, "Swim for the music that saves you when you're not so sure you'll survive... Swim for your family, your lovers, your sisters and brothers and friends." And I did. I'm proud to say that I did survive it, and things are going better than ever. Life is starting again, and I feel fantastic!

I got to meet the lead singer of Jack's Mannequin, Andrew McMahon, last year shortly after starting peritoneal dialysis. I got to tell him how much his music meant to me and how it essentially saved my life. He understood because he himself had done battle with acute lymphatic leukemia and won! Perhaps that's why he knew just the words to write to get me through those dark times; he was a kindred spirit. The hug I got from him will stick with me for the rest of my life, and the impact he and his music have had on me is probably greater than anyone could understand.

I know that more trying times are ahead. Chronic kidney disease isn't an easy road to walk, and there are bound to be many more hurdles to overcome. But as long as I remember to keep swimming and keep my head above water, I know I'll make it through. I've always said that I've learned the greatest lessons in life from music. In the words of Andrew McMahon: "I swim for brighter days despite the absence of sun, choking on salt water. I'm not giving in, I swim."

Somewhere Between Life and Death

Mary Wu

I WAS ALWAYS THE AVID bookworm, with my tinted-framed glasses perched on the end of my nose, my head buried in the book I was devouring, and my eyes glazed over with a dreamy glint. Books were my ultimate escape from the realities of my kidney failure and one disastrous health episode after another since I was a tiny toddler. For a little while, I could get lost and wrapped up in the magic, imagination, and creativity of the author, the characters, and the plot that thickened with each page.

Books became even more my best friend when I was 12 years old and was told that my first kidney transplant had only 10% function remaining. The author I turned to each and every time I had another blood test or nephrologist visit was Lurlene McDaniel: her book with the binding tattered and the cover bent was "Somewhere Between Life and Death."

To briefly summarize, the book focuses on two sisters, Amy and Erin. Erin grew up envious of Amy's carefree and happy ways.

When Amy dies in a tragic car accident, the real story starts, with the entire organ donation process, the complex family dynamics before a loved one dies and after making the ultimate decision to donate the organs at a tragic time, and the never-ending raw and challenging emotions that are experienced throughout it all.

> Like a warm blanket wrapped around me on a frigid, wintry night, or a steaming, hot bowl of chicken noodle soup, the book provided comfort for me.

It was strange that I turned to this book and read it endlessly because it was realistic and true to my own personal and health experience rather than providing an unrealistic fantasy world that I could run away to when times were tough.

Growing up with chronic kidney failure wasn't easy for my family and me. There was the sibling rivalry that my sister and I had that mirrored Amy and Erin's to capture the constant love and attention of our parents. There were the protective and loving parents who were beside themselves with the unknown future both in my life and in this treasured book. There was the uncertainty of whether I would receive a second kidney transplant in time or undergo dialysis again, or what life held for me. This was similar for Erin, who confronted a future without her sister and those organs that were to be given mysteriously to faceless strangers.

Each time I read this book, I knew deep in my heart why I loved and held on to it like an anchor. Like a warm blanket wrapped around me on a frigid, wintry night or a steaming, hot bowl of chicken noodle soup, the book provided comfort for me. I learned about the organ donation process, the triumphs and heartaches of the donor family, and most of all, I learned and felt deep within me that I wasn't alone. This author understood my family and our turmoil all too well. Furthermore, as a candidate waiting for my second kidney transplant and chance at life again, I understood that there was no reason for me to feel bitter, angry, or lonely because this book made me see the other side—the side of the organ donor's family.

When I was able to step back from my own situation, a deep understanding penetrated and filled me with calmness and happiness that were unexplainable and wonderful all at once: I understood that an organ donor's family or organ recipient's family didn't matter and never did matter. Instead, what it came down to was that all of us as human beings are survivors who face and overcome life's greatest struggles and challenges in the best and only way that we know how.

A small paperback book gave me the strength and understanding to deal with my chronic kidney failure and with waiting to see what life had in store for me either with another kidney transplant or with dialysis—overcoming the hormones and loneliness that hit me full throttle in high school and treasuring my life as it was and my family as they were. A small paperback book was there for me when I did eventually receive my second kidney transplant, helping me to treasure my organ donor and her family as though they were my very own. One small paperback book made all the difference in the world to me, and I could never thank this author and this tattered book enough for all of that and all of the lessons I learned from it.

A Cheerful Heart and a Good Report

Susan Decuir

"A cheerful heart does good like medicine," from my favorite book, encouraged me to get going and meet my daughter and grandchildren at the pool that day last summer. Though hereditary polycystic kidney disease had slowed me down, I had a lot of living to do yet. Besides, snuggle-bug hugs and wet kisses from my grandbabies always cheer me up. No retiring to a rocking chair or feeling sorry for myself for this Nana! Besides, I love the water.

Tugging my hand, 3-year-old Evan begged, "Slide with me, Nana." Like a trained puppy, I obediently followed, wading through the mass of animated children visiting the city pool that steamy June afternoon.

Winded, as usual, after climbing steps, I paused at the top to catch my breath. "It's our turn, Nana." Evan's sky-blue eyes sparkled with excitement. I positioned Evan on my lap and wrapped my arms tightly around his waist. "Ready?" I asked.

"Ready, Nana."

"Whee!" I squealed, pushing off into the dark, winding tunnel. Is that me giggling? Around the bend we flew, cool water surrounding us, then splash! We landed in a heap in the refreshing pool.

"That was fun, Nana."

"Let's go again," I said.

"Mom, are you sure?"

My daughter's concern was more about my having been placed on the transplant list two months earlier—dialysis imminent with 8% kidney function—than about the sinus infection I'd battled for two weeks, on the second round of antibiotics.

I truly felt wonderful.
Cheerful.

"I'm fine," I beamed. I truly felt wonderful. Cheerful.

"One more time, then I'll watch the baby for you," I promised.

Several days later, my heart sank when my vascular surgeon said that a third surgery was needed to complete my fistula. My husband and I had plans to attend a friend's out-of-town wedding on the Fourth of July. "Think on things that are a good report," popped into my thoughts, a line from the book.

"Surely it can wait till after the July Fourth weekend," I said with amazing boldness. "Besides, I'm still believing in a miracle, and just maybe I'll never have to go on dialysis." He smirked; I smiled, clinging to a favorite line from the book: "Faith is the substance of things hoped for, the evidence of things not seen."

I bought my dress; Ron made hotel reservations.

The week before the wedding I was relaxing on my recliner on a quiet Saturday afternoon when the phone rang. A glance at the caller ID indicated a Texas number. "Telemarketer," I grumbled. "I'm not answering." Suddenly, an inner voice boomed, "Answer this call."

"Hi, this is Heather from Methodist Transplant with good news. We have a perfect kidney match for you." My body started shaking. Am I still breathing? I've been on the list for only two months. "What did you say?" I asked, pushing myself off the recliner to find my husband. After recovering from the initial shock, we called our daughter, prayed, then headed for the hospital, a peace that passes all understanding surrounding us.

The staff treated me like royalty. Testing proved that my health was good and that miraculously no trace of antibiotics was left in my system.

When I was told that the surgeon I'd hoped for, my brother's transplant surgeon 12 years earlier, was out of town for the weekend, Ron and I began to pray. The book says, "You have not because you ask not." We asked. Within the hour, the surgeon walked into my room. "I decided to come home early," he grinned.

The same peace I felt from the moment I received Heather's call surrounded me throughout the transplant process. My quick recovery amazed everyone; I was ready to go home four days after surgery. Heather came to see me off. Beaming, she said, "It's not often I get to say we have a perfect match. Your donor could have been your twin." I wiped away a tear. We hugged.

Every day I thank God for my miracle and for the stranger with a heart big enough to think of others by signing a donor card—something I've done since my transplant.

In honor of my donor and his or her family, I strive to stay healthy by following my doctor's instructions, exercising, eating well, and taking my meds.

It's summer again, and this year 2-year-old Emma and 4-year-old Evan take turns on the water slide with their new and improved Nana; I'm feeling fantastic and having the time of my life. My favorite book—the Bible.

I Will Not Be Moved

Jasmine Davis

WHEN I WAS 6 YEARS OLD, I never would have imagined that I'd be sick. I have a disease called lupus nephritis, an inflammation of the kidney caused by systemic lupus erythematosus (SLE), a disease of the immune system. SLE usually causes harm to the skin, joints, kidneys, and brain. Luckily for me, it didn't harm my brain or my skin or joints, but my kidneys instead. From the time I was 6 to the age I am now—15—I've taken numerous pills to keep my lupus under control. I've been through chemotherapy and all kinds of treatments that might help my kidney disease. When everything seems hopeless, I pray and listen to 89.3 KSBJ.

Many songs touch my heart; however, one song is my favorite: "Will Not Be Moved" by Natalie Grant. This song says that you might stumble or fall down, but you won't be moved. I can relate to this because this song tells me that I'll go through problems, and it'll get hard, yet it's up to me to persevere. Without my faith in the Lord and my family on my side, I wouldn't be as strong as I am.

When no one is listening and I'm ready to give up, the Lord shows me that He hasn't forgotten me.

When I was 12 years old, my lupus went out of control, and my kidneys shut down. Now I dialyze three times a week at Texas Children's Hospital in Houston. In the beginning, I felt like the world was coming to an end. I kept asking myself, "What have I done to deserve this?" I lost weight, couldn't keep nutrients down, and wasn't able to go to school. The doctors thought I'd need a feeding tube. I was in the hospital for three months. The doctors lost all hope, telling my mother that I might not make it.

My mother started to pray and put oil on my head. She played gospel music in the room. While listening to the music, I started to have more strength. Later, I was able to keep food down and to gain weight. My labs improved, shocking the doctors, but not my mother and me.

It was a miracle.

> In the beginning, I felt like the world was coming to an end.

I've had countless surgeries. I had a catheter in my chest to do treatments. My sacred body was invaded and painful. With the catheter, I wasn't able to have a life. The line mustn't get wet, so when I'd bathe, I'd cover the catheter with shields called Aqua Guards. I didn't like it. I have a fistula now, inside my arm. With this, I can do anything. I swim, sweat, and play as I want. I can be normal.

When your kidneys shut down, you're limited in the amount of fluid you can have, and you have to balance your calcium, phosphorus, and potassium. You'd think with having to go to school, take my medicine, and do homework that I would have given up, but my song, "Will Not Be Moved," helps me and motivates me to keep going.

I must work even harder in school than others to show that I belong. I try to do work and projects ahead of time since I never know when I'm going to be sick. I focus on my courses and study so much. My teachers tell me that they wish they had more students like me, students who are determined. At school, sometimes I'm bullied, but I ignore my peers. I have days when I'm sad and happy. I do wish for more friends and to be normal some days. When I'm like this, I start to pray and talk to my mother, and she tells me that this too shall pass.

Right now, I'm on dialysis, but later on I won't be. I'll have my kidney transplant, and I'll be able to have a normal life. I'll be able to go shopping and eat and drink whatever I want, whenever I want. Right now, I just have to have faith and know that my time is coming. Just like the song says, I'll keep on going and never give up.

I Will Survive

Terri Waddell

I LOVE MUSIC. Music has always been an important part of my life. It's helped me deal with all of the situations that have occurred in my life, both good and bad. So it just seemed natural that I'd again turn to music to deal with one of the most difficult situations that I've ever had to deal with: kidney disease and dialysis.

When I was pregnant with my third child, I started having problems with my kidneys. By the time my daughter was two years old, I had end-stage renal disease and was starting dialysis. The music that I listened to has taught me many lessons when it comes to dealing with dialysis. However, there are four songs that I feel have taught me the most important lessons in regard to dealing with chronic kidney disease and dialysis.

The first and most important lesson that I learned is that "I Will Survive." This is a song by Gloria Gaynor. I know that in the song she's talking about a man, but so many of the words parallel exactly what I was feeling at the time. The song starts out saying,

"At first I was afraid, I was petrified," which was exactly how I felt. I was so scared that I wouldn't live to see my three children grow up. I was afraid that my whole life would change. There's another part of the song that says, "It took all the strength I had not to fall apart." It also says, "I used to cry, but now I hold my head up high." Those words definitely described me when I first found out that I had kidney disease. I was just trying to deal with things and not fall apart. I cried all the time, but I now know that I can deal with this kidney disease: "I hold my head up high." The most important lesson that I learned from this song is that I will survive. As long as I continue to follow my doctor's guidance and come to dialysis regularly, I'll survive and thrive.

> I know that God has carried me through and that without Him, I wouldn't have made it.

The second lesson that I learned came from two songs: "We Are Family" by Sister Sledge and "With A Little Help From My Friends" by the Beatles. I found out how important the support of my family and friends was throughout this process. In the beginning, I was sick and spent a lot of time in the hospital. My family would take my children and make sure that they were well cared for when I couldn't take care of them myself. My friends would not only encourage me, but they would come over and help my children and me. They were willing to help do the things that I couldn't do at the time. I don't know what I would have done without the love and support that were shown to me by my family and friends.

The last lesson I learned as I've gone through this journey was the importance of my faith. The song that reminds me of this is called "Never Would Have Made It" by Marvin Sapp. The song says, "I made it through my storms and my test because you were there to carry me through my mess." I know that God has carried me through and that without Him, I wouldn't have made it.

I've seen all of my children graduate from high school, and now they're working on accomplishing their goals. I'm so grateful that God has blessed me, and I know that it is He who has kept me. Just like the words of the song, I can say that "I am stronger, I am wiser, I am better, much better." I made it. I don't know what the future holds for me, but right now I can say that I never would have made it as far as I did without God in my life.

So these are the lessons that I've learned through songs. They've helped me deal with my kidney disease in a way that has been positive and uplifting. I'm sure that I'll have many more challenges throughout the rest of my life, and there's one thing I can be sure of: music will continue to help me through these challenges.

"Man's Search for Meaning"

Lawrence Wildman

THE SEDATIVE WAS WEARING OFF, and I could see that my left foot hadn't been amputated. The good news was that the operation to treat the infected bones in my ankle was a success; the bad news was that after many years of recurrent kidney stone damage, my kidneys had failed. Overnight. I became a hemodialysis patient. I didn't void very much and had to learn to control my fluid intake, as well as adopt food restrictions to lessen the intake of substances that my body couldn't easily remove.

The next month passed slowly, as I regained strength and tried to understand what my new life would be like. I'd just returned to the city to start a master's degree in information studies, after spending a few years in my home town caring for my sick mother and grandmother. They'd both passed away in the same year, leaving me divorced and childless and with no immediate family.

My friends were very supportive, but had busy, full lives of their own. I'd have to find some additional means of support to help me deal with this strange new life. Circumstances prevented me from returning to graduate school, but as a former teacher, I yearned for some intellectual outlet. I learned of a humanities course sponsored by local universities; this soon became a regular part of my life. I renewed my love of classical literature.

One of my professors knew of my medical condition and suggested a book that had helped him gain perspective when life's trials occurred. This was "Man's Search for Meaning: An Introduction to Logotherapy" by Viktor E. Frankl. The book, although only 163 pages long, is a formidable piece of work. It consists of two parts: the first recounts his experiences as a concentration camp inmate, while the second is an examination of the ideas of meaning and his theory of logotherapy.

That isn't to say that I'm in any way equating my disease with the horrors of Nazi Germany and the suffering endured by millions of people. However, I do find some empathy with Frankl. We both have had suffering and disease forced on us by factors outside our control; our happiness and even survival may seem unlikely at times, and there's no immediate, foreseeable end to our plight. So if Frankl can find a way to survive the soul-destroying experiences of a concentration camp, surely I can use his inspiration to handle my own struggle, meager as it may seem in comparison!

Early in his writing, Frankl emphasizes that his story is uniquely his own and that each prisoner has his own particular road to travel. I've found this to be true in considering chronic kidney disease. I can relate to the plight of other patients and try to help them learn from my experiences, but ultimately one must take one's own road to acceptance, endurance, and, hopefully, survival and recovery.

> ...the meaning of life is found not in any dramatic act, but rather in every moment of living...

The question remains: How has this book helped me with my own trials and challenges of renal disease and dialysis? Frankl theorizes that the meaning of life is found not in any dramatic act, but rather in every moment of living; life never ceases to have meaning, even in the face of suffering. Further, he feels that for everyone in a dire condition, there's someone looking down—a friend, a family member, or even God, who would expect not to be disappointed. Thus, even when we feel at our most alone and vulnerable, we must try to live up to the expectations of those whose love we value. He states this most eloquently and succinctly when he writes: "The salvation of man is through love and in love."

Finally, there's one passage among many that has helped me in my ongoing fight:

> It did not really matter what we expected from life, but rather what life expected from us. We needed to stop asking about

the meaning of life, and instead to think of ourselves as those who were being questioned by life daily and hourly. Our answer must consist not in talk and meditation, but in right action and in right conduct. Life ultimately means taking the responsibility to find the right answer to its problems and to fulfill the tasks which it constantly sets for each individual.

Not a bad message to send across the generations.

The Art of Living

Rita Knight-Gray

I WAS HIT BY END-STAGE RENAL DISEASE in late December 2004. Previously I'd been told that my kidneys were operating at 50%; I still felt good, even though my shoulders and neck continually pained me and I had to adjust to my low energy level. When I went to the doctor to see if my neck pain could be alleviated, blood tests indicated that my kidneys had failed and that I needed dialysis. It was December 31 and I had tickets to a New Year's Eve party, but instead of going, I was getting a catheter and having dialysis all in one day. This is not how I wanted 2005 to begin; there wasn't any warning. I couldn't believe that this was happening to me, Miss Eat-Healthy-Get-Enough-Sleep-Exercise-Right-Girl.

I was in complete denial, and being a librarian, I had to research my situation and find out why this had happened to me. I was on my research quest for all of 2005 when I stumbled on the Dalai Lama's book "The Art of Happiness: A Handbook for Living." You must understand that I read for research; I don't read much for pleasure. Being a videographer, I'm really into pictures. But this book has a great way of breaking down the various ways you should approach life in terms of your happiness. Even though I'd become interested in Buddhism, I wasn't sure what to expect from this book. As I browsed through it, the chapter on facing suffering grabbed my attention. Some of the Buddhist teachings had given me some insight regarding my feelings of denial, but for me it wasn't enough.

> ...being a librarian, I had to research my situation and find out why this had happened to me.

The first anecdote in the chapter was about Kisagotami, a mother whose son died and who asked Buddha to bring him back to life. Buddha told her that it could be done; all that was needed was mustard seeds from a household that didn't experience any deaths. Kisagotami searched and searched, and what she found was that in every household a death had occurred. She learned from this experience that she wasn't alone in suffering the death of someone. Buddha explained to her that some type of suffering is a part of everyone's life.

The Dalai Lama stated that his personal way of tolerating suffering is to understand Samsara, an endless cycle of life, death, and rebirth—that the ordinary state of day-to-day existence is formed by our negative and positive actions. Once the negative thoughts and actions are removed, the mind can achieve a state of liberation.

When I observed the various people having dialysis and discussed with them how their kidneys had failed and the other health problems they had to contend with, I found that I wasn't alone and that my kidney problem wasn't that bad. Aside from my failed kidneys, I still had my health. I could eat most of the foods I liked, dance, travel, and exercise. Life wasn't bad: it was a Samsara, and by thinking positively, I was able to liberate myself from the negative pain of denial.

2011 Essay Theme

What hobby helps improve
your quality of life
and helps you forget
the many challenges
kidney disease presents?

A Breath of Fresh Air

Valen Cover

I'M THANKFUL FOR the vast number of hospital memories that have been tucked away in a box, in the bottom shelf of a dresser drawer, down a long hallway, in the back of my mind. However, if I close my eyes, there are some memories I can retrieve instantly and relive the moment.

In 2002, I was lying on a gurney, ready to be taken for another operation. I'd been in the hospital for several months, and my tiny veins couldn't handle the daily blood draws. A port was put in my neck so blood could be drawn more easily. I was accustomed to being pushed through the cold, dark hallways of Johns Hopkins, from one building to another, hearing the wheels squeak in the quiet hallways and feeling every bump along the way. The usual view was the plain ceiling and cement walls. However, one day my father asked the transport service, "Is there any way we can get her some fresh air?" They paused and said, "Sure—we can go a different way today."

Off we went down the hall, turning left, then right, and straight ahead for a long time. All of a sudden I heard the noise of a door opening, and my view of the plain ceiling was transformed into a gorgeous blue sky, with puffy clouds. A cool breeze blew across my face. I felt alive. This breath of fresh air was the medicine I needed. As fast as the freedom arrived, it vanished as we entered the next building. That day I experienced a feeling that I embraced, a sensation that gave me hope, that let my imagination run wild. It was an emotion that led me to my love of the great outdoors.

Whether you've had a bad day at work, or like me, have been battling polycystic kidney disease from an early age, we all need a breath of fresh air, an escape from reality. Today, my escape is hiking in the great outdoors.

This year I hiked the tallest waterfall trail in the United States and the second tallest in the world: Yosemite Falls. I never underestimate what our bodies can endure. I spent 11 months in the hospital when I was 19 and 20 and both my kidneys were removed. I was on dialysis and thankfully received a kidney transplant. I believe there's nothing I can't overcome.

As I hiked 2,425 feet up Yosemite Falls, I didn't think of the challenges I face on a daily basis due to kidney disease. Instead, I felt empowered. Hiking has improved my quality of life, not only physically but mentally. It's vital to always have something to look forward to and set goals and achieve them. As my fiancé and I got ready to climb up the granite cliff, I stood at the bottom and giggled and thought: "I'm going to hike to the top of that!" The journey to the top was difficult, with constant uphill grades and switchbacks; however, the perfect blue sky and sunshine kept me focused and determined to reach my goal. Adventures like this contain mysterious, hidden treasures along the way, and breathtaking views become snapshots in your mind.

> It's vital to always have something to look forward to and set goals and achieve them.

My favorite moment occurred when I reached the top of the mountain and looked down to see how small everything was and how far I'd traveled. I looked at the mountains in the distance and my mind was clear, my imagination soared, and I was hopeful for my future. I took my 2:00 p.m. transplant meds at the top of Yosemite Falls, filled with sheer joy, proud of my accomplishment, and overwhelmed with the beauty of transplantation and what I'm able to do today thanks to the gift I've been given.

When I'm enjoying nature, life seems clearer to me. I consume the simple beauties of the world, re-energized. I reflect on what really matters and dream about the great future ahead of me. I felt like I was on top of the world, standing at the summit of Yosemite Falls. Birds soared at eye level, and I was engulfed by a calm, peaceful feeling that told me: "Everything is going to be okay." I reflected on my life and how far I've come and how far I plan on going. Living with kidney disease isn't easy, but I'm proud to say that I'm not only surviving, I'm thriving!

She's Gone to Pot

Ellen Sonenthal

SHE'S GONE TO POT! What's your first thought when you read this? Someone is crazy, has let herself go, is smoking an illegal substance (in most states), or has a hobby that involves a pottery wheel, clay, and creativity. In my case, it's the last one.

When I was a child, we went to lots of Midwest art fairs. My parents always knew that I'd gravitate to the pottery, especially if there was a demonstration. I was mesmerized by the motion of the wheel and the elegance of the forms that would be "thrown" on it. Wow! I could watch for hours and often did. Best of all, this was a free activity, an important factor when you're poor.

After my college graduation, I vowed that I'd learn to throw pots. And I did. It lived up to my expectations. Taking a ball of clay and turning it into a usable vessel was thrilling! My first pots were—well, first pots. But you have to start somewhere.

For years, I told everyone that pottery classes were for stress management and definitely cheaper than therapy! Also, I ended up with lots of bowls that I enjoy using daily. Then, late last year (2010), it became increasingly difficult for me to find the strength and stamina to make pottery. Much to my shock, I was diagnosed with end-stage renal failure. Depression set in, and my stress management tool wasn't available to me.

In late December, I was in the emergency room to start dialysis. At first, I really didn't feel much better, but as I inched toward my dry weight, I started to feel better and get my strength back. Every week, I went to the pottery studio—sometimes I just went to chat and see the demonstrations, sometimes I'd find simple projects to complete, but it was always the one thing that I really looked forward to.

> I could throw again,
> and all was right with the world.

After the placement of my fistula, I had less strength in my arm. But I persevered. I asked others to get my clay down and replace it when I was finished, since I couldn't lift the 25 pounds. Slowly but surely I've gained more and more abilities as my fistula has matured. My pottery isn't as elegant and accomplished as it was before, but I can do a lot and I can trim to get the right shapes. I could throw again, and all was right with the world. Once again, I was mesmerized by the movement of the wheel, as

I was during my childhood.

Most of my bowls are donated to the "Empty Bowl Project"; this is a nationwide initiative of American potters to help feed the homeless. All bowls are donated and then sold to the public for $16. The bowls are washed, and then you can choose a soup you'd like to eat. In Las Vegas, there are silent and live auctions as well. Last year, we raised a little over $42,000!

Now, my hobby of taking a lump of clay and throwing it into a functional bowl is not only a hobby, but also a stress management tool and my salvation once again. It helps me feel normal and alive, instead of just a dialysis patient! When I'm in class, I'm a potter and proud of it!

Music Moves Me

Gary Severson

WHEN I WAS 10, I persuaded my mom to let me take piano lessons so I could play the popular songs I heard on the radio. Afterward I was shocked to find out that I needed to practice each day to play those songs. Bye-bye, piano. The following Christmas, my mom bought me an acoustic guitar so I could become the next Elvis. I looked cool standing in front of our mirror, holding my guitar and wiggling my right thigh. But I could never even strum the guitar properly. Bye-bye, guitar.

Listening to music has always interested me. In the late 1960s I was a dialysis patient, and I listened to rock music while I dialyzed. The dialysis runs were quite long back then, and I certainly didn't want to spend all of my time doing school work!

Music speaks to people in different ways. For instance, many songs that I heard while on dialysis affected me emotionally. Today when I hear those songs, sometimes I'm reminded of when they first captivated me. I can still repeat the melodies and lyrics of many Beatles songs.

Forty years ago, I received my kidney transplant and began investigating many types of music: Christian, Big Band, jazz, and even classical. After hearing Jimmy Dorsey play, I decided that I too would play the alto sax. I bought a student's model and took lessons for four months. Then came the harder work of improving my sound and learning to play by ear. For 15 years, my wife (on piano) and I made music together for an hour each week. I believe that I've finally become an accomplished beginner.

One night, I heard an enchanting melody in a dream. When I woke up, I thought that someone needed to write down that melody. The next night I had the same dream. This time when I awakened, I knew who that someone was. I fumbled on the piano for days until I got the melody down. Next I needed chords and words. Words weren't too difficult, since I'd written articles and stories, but chords—eek! So I enlisted my wife to instruct me. She taught me about chords in one session, but it required years of trying and failing and trying once more before I ever dared use my songs in public or give one as a gift. Even now, only on my good days am I near average in writing and playing songs.

So if my labor of love turns out to be mostly labor, why do it at all? Well, it keeps the focus off my kidney problems. For years, periods of high blood pressure and nights of poor sleep acted like we were best friends. I had to force myself to compose songs. But I've found that even when my body demands attention, if I play an instrument or sing (again, average is good for me), there's an up-lifting of the spirit. In other words, music can at least momentarily help me transcend my kidney difficulties.

This past decade, stents were put in my kidney artery to lower my blood pressure. That brought 2½ years of daily problems with widely fluctuating blood pressure. Yet during that time, I began playing three different hand drums, a number of hand instruments, and the harmonica—all of them while sitting down to compensate for any blood pressure craziness.

> Music can at least momentarily help me transcend my kidney difficulties.

I've also discovered that playing an instrument or singing can lower my blood pressure. I believe the secret is that those actions ease stress, which makes for lower blood pressure readings. On many occasions, I've sung to my blood pressure to coax it to return to normal, and sometimes it does! But even beyond that, music brings me joy and keeps me positive. It's become a creative outlet without bad side effects.

In my journey as a kidney patient. I've experienced increased pain, trouble with walking, and greater fatigue "drops" in the eve-nings. However, since mornings are best for me, my wife and I lead worship at two prayer meetings each week at a nearby prayer center.

Despite the possible physical struggle to get to the meetings, they're the highlight of our day. Call me stubborn, call me stupid, but I don't want to kick the music habit!

For the Love of Cooking

Versie McCullough

I KNEW MY KIDNEYS were failing. It was apparent several years before my doctor informed me that I would need dialysis or die. That was one of the worst days of my life. I was devastated. I thought to myself—go to the same place, three days a week, four hours a day, needles stuck in me, a machine acting as an artificial kidney, I might as well be dead! What quality of life could I have?

After a few months of having "pity parties," I examined all aspects of my life, not just the kidney disease. I decided, "I have so much to live for!" I had three children and two granddaughters (now I have four granddaughters). While they're enough to live for, I began to ask myself, "What do I love to do that would improve my quality of life and help me forget the many challenges kidney disease is about to present for me?" I decided to put all my energy into what I enjoy doing most: cooking.

Over the years, I've collected over 20 cookbooks and subscribed to many magazines with recipes. I like to watch the Cooking Channel, which is my Saturday pastime during treatment.

Why cooking? The challenges during and after treatment such as cramping, dizziness, nausea, weakness, and lack of energy can quickly change my outlook. Cooking helps keep my mind focused. While dialyzing, I think about the food I can provide to tickle my family's taste buds. I make the best of my treatment time. My memory isn't as sharp as it once was, so I try to commit recipes to memory or think of new ways I can improve the recipes I already know. Cooking allows me to make different foods for others, foods I can no longer enjoy because of the disease.

> ## In spite of the challenges,
> ## I choose to cook and I choose to live.

I like introducing my grandchildren to the foods my mother cooked when I was young. I remember getting off the bus and smelling freshly baked tea cakes from my mother's kitchen. Fond memories help me forget the challenges. Today, tea cakes are one of my favorite items to make for family and friends. Cooking is a great opportunity to teach history and heritage. My granddaughters had no idea what tea cakes were. One thought it was a cake you eat with tea. My mother gave me her recipe years ago. My girls won't allow me to share it with anyone (very selfish, don't you think?).

People are always requesting tea cakes. To cheer up my friends at dialysis, I often cook my tea cakes to bring to them. One of the patients thinks I buy them at the bakery. However, I reassure everyone that the tea cakes are my own.

Recently, I faced a problem with circulation in my hand and began experiencing extreme hypotension (low blood pressure). This is common in people on dialysis. Several times I've passed out because of hypotension. Did it stop me from cooking? Definitely not. I'm blessed with a walker, the type with a seat attached. When I feel lightheaded, I take the walker to the kitchen, sit on the seat, and go for it.

I continue to face more challenges. Within the last year, I had a cancerous kidney removed. I continue to cook. My stand mixer broke, so now I rely on my hand mixer. I'm hoping to receive a stand mixer from Santa this Christmas.

I've learned that dialysis is not a death sentence. I spend my 12 hours a week contemplating what I can cook and forgetting the challenges that kidney disease presents. I plan to continue cooking as long as I have life.

It's been over a 12-year journey with kidney disease. I started dialysis in March 1999. Now, it's been 12¼ years, 148 months, 640 weeks, 1,920 days, 7,680 hours, and lots of friends lost along this journey. In spite of the challenges, I choose to cook and I choose to live.

So if you're shopping in the grocery store one day and see a delightful dessert called "Vee's Tea Cakes," make sure you try them: they could be mine.

Let Go and Play

Kelly Chuba

AFTER TEN YEARS of gradual decline, my kidneys failed last year. Soon I'll mark my first anniversary on home dialysis. Thanks largely to the freedom of home dialysis, I've been able to pursue a few different hobbies—hobbies I chose carefully largely by looking back at the things that gave me the most pleasure in my youth. So while I'm a woman who's just turned 40, I think I may just now be an old teenager, but with good reason. After feeling sad and lost, I decided that instead of letting dialysis make me old and sick, I was going to be young again, and being young again means doing some very youthful things.

In my adventure to recapture my youth, I decided to go back to the job I enjoyed the most in my life: amusement park security. It's not an easy job for a dialysis patient, but it's wonderful exercise in the fresh air and sunshine, with happy people in one of the greatest playgrounds on earth: Hershey Park. Today I rode the old carousel, which was built almost a hundred years ago. I chose one of the elaborately decorated wooden horses that I had to climb up to reach, and for a few short minutes, like many generations before me, I was very small and carefree again. I'm free to get on any of the rides, although my doctors tell me to avoid the big roller coasters. I have to remind myself that the posted warnings for people with medical conditions actually mean me. Fortunately, we have a mild coaster called the Trailblazer. I rode that today too.

Before I left for work, I played a few very intense games of StarCraft II on my laptop. StarCraft is a real-time strategy game that requires lightning-fast reactions and quick decisions to save the armies we command. I often play this game while on dialysis, because like most good video games, StarCraft can make time disappear while stimulating the pleasure center of our brains. They say video games are addictive, and I believe them! I wish that everyone in dialysis centers had video games during those long treatments. From Slingo to Zombie Oblivion, there really is a fun game for everyone!

Sometimes I don't feel very good on dialysis, so I put on the television programs the kids like. I don't really care to watch the upsetting adult shows like crime dramas or the news; I much prefer the better, gentler world of Nickelodeon. I know that many grown-ups also enjoy these cartoons but deny themselves because of what other grown-ups might think. I've put away the disturbing books in my library and read all of the Newberry Award classics and the Harry Potter series instead. Reclaiming our youth means no longer denying healthy activities we would enjoy just because other adults have a notion of what we should be reading or watching.

> After feeling sad and lost,
> I decided that instead of letting
> dialysis make me old and sick,
> I was going to be young again.

Last spring I was kicked out of our under-30 softball league when someone squealed and told them I was older. Sadly, before I could join an age-appropriate league, the nice doctors put a fistula in my right arm, ending my softball career. But this fall I plan to find a kickball league. I'll need the stress-reducing exercise and the camaraderie of teammates when our amusement park closes for the season.

Exercise is a great way to reclaim our youth, and while last year I started with just walking my dogs, before long I got stronger and could eventually run and swim. This fall, I also plan to dress for Halloween, find my way out of a corn maze, and go to homecoming at my military college. When Christmas comes, I'll go caroling, and spring will mean coloring Easter eggs. With luck, next summer I'll go swimming more and try to travel with my home dialysis machine.

My hobbies are the joys of my youth, and I fully endorse the hobby of reclaiming our youth. Yes, I have to pause to stick myself with needles and obey a beeping machine for three hours a day, but how much more fun life is when we just let go and play!

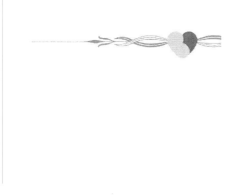

My Life with Clorox

Jasmine Davis

SINCE I WAS BORN, Clorox Wipes have always been in my life. From the time I learned to walk and talk, if my mom was cleaning, I remember her using Clorox. I learned a lot from my mom, so later on, when I was older and able to use Clorox myself, I'd do exactly what she did: wipe the counters, clean my bathroom and my bedroom, sanitize the dishes and anything else I could get my hands on. I'd found something that I enjoyed: cleaning.

Most people don't enjoy cleaning. I often hear people say to me, "Oh, I need to take you home to my house," or "Why do you like to clean so much?" I can say that not only do I like cleaning, but refreshing spaces with Clorox takes my mind off things, like when I'm stressed out about bad results from the hospital. Clorox Wipes reveal in me the cleanliness and pride I take in things.

Most people have something they do that makes them happy, and cleaning is my thing.

Every other weekend, I go to Walmart or any other grocery

store and buy liquid Clorox and Clorox Wipes unless I already have them. I use other cleaning products as well, like dish detergent, Tide, Snuggles, and Dawn, but for some reason, Clorox, to me, is the best. When I'm finished cleaning with Clorox, the rooms feel and smell clean. I can tell if I haven't cleaned a room with Clorox.

> Most people have something
> they do that makes them happy,
> and cleaning is my thing.

I've always made sure that everything is clean, although since I'm getting older, I'm more cautious about dirt, especially in the hospital where I receive dialysis three times a week. In 2006, my kidneys shut down, and I had to go on dialysis. You'd think that the hospital would be a clean place, but from my experience, it's the opposite.

When I first found out that I had to go on dialysis, I was emotionally, physically, and spiritually weakened by the news. My mom made sure that I was fed and clean and that my room was wiped down with Clorox. One time I was admitted to the hospital, and the staff said that they'd cleaned my room. My mother went into the room before me and came and told the nurses that it wasn't clean. She immediately started wiping counters down and showing them the filth. She kept on cleaning until the cleaning people came back. We both watched them as they cleaned. I have to thank God that I have my mother, because without her I'm pretty sure that I'd be even sicker than I am now. She speaks up in my defense, and she keeps my life and spaces tidy and clean.

Every time I go into the dialysis unit, I have Clorox Wipes in a small bag with some clothes that I change into, and before I get on my machine, I wipe down whatever I might touch, like my dialysis chair, my television, my hospital phone, and the visitor's chair. When I have surgeries and am very weak from all the medicines the surgeon has given me, my mother comes and she wipes down whatever I can't do.

People might say that I'm a neat freak when they see me with my Clorox Wipes, but I don't care. I'd rather people feel that way about me than get sick from so many germs and bacteria. I'm not like regular kids. When I use Clorox Wipes, I'm transported to a whole new world. I know that I can't control my kidney disease, but I can control what kinds of germs and bacteria are around me by wiping them away with Clorox. My immune system is very weak, and I'll do whatever I have to do to make sure that I don't get sick.

Clorox Wipes have been in my family for many, many years. They've been on many journeys with me—journeys when I was happy, sad, or angry—and I plan to use them in the future.

The Odd Ones

Keith Matthews

Question: "What hobby helps improve your quality of life and helps you forget the many challenges kidney disease presents?"

Answer: When I arrive at the DCI Clinic in Crowley, Louisiana, the staff always gives me a friendly greeting, but makes no move to start my treatment for the first several minutes.

Why not? Because I'm one of "them."

The Odd Ones.

Oh, don't pretend that you don't know what I'm talking about. Every clinic, in fact, every patient shift, has at least one Odd One. We come in different colors, shapes, and sizes, and our eccentricities are as immediately recognizable as the ringtone on our teenager's cell phone.

From Ms. Mary's garlic-sardine radish salad every Monday, Wednesday, and Friday (made fresh every Sunday), to Papa Joe's noisy domino game ("Big Six! Now take that!"), played solo on the chair-side table, our oddities and profundities are the stuff of legend.

We see you, we Odd Ones, when we walk in, looking over your eyeglasses at us. You're hoping against all hope that some-how, somehow, during our day off, we've been converted from the mad eccentricity that possesses us. But in the words of New Jersey hit man Vito the Enforcer, "Fuggeddaboudit."

Why, you may wonder, are we so strange? Why do we insist on clinging to our quirks, our anomalies, our…our…oh, just say it—our kookiness?

I'll tell you.

No matter how long we've been on hemodialysis, no mat-ter how many times we've smelled the antiseptic and heard the whirrs and clicks and soft beeps of the machinery, it still bothers us more than we care to admit. It's not really the needles or the sight of so much of our blood leaving our body…

…well, that is a bit creepy.…

But I digress.

It's knowing that what once was a simple matter of five minutes and a quick flush in a bathroom stall is now a process—a process that takes 3½ (frickin'!!!) hours, involving people we probably wouldn't trust not to squirt the last of the liquid soap in a public restroom, inserting needles in our arms with the oft-told lie, "A little stick!"

Yeah, right.

It's not knowing when our access will clot off and we'll have to go to the ER and wait for hours, hoping that the surgeon who'll fix the problem isn't as wet behind the ears as the bubblegum he's chewing would indicate.

> I write because that sets me free from the chains that masquerade as tubes.

It's knowing that barring a miracle, the rest of our lives will revolve around a reclining chair and a quarter-ton rectangular box that's designed for the sole purpose of taking our blood on a sterile, macabre roller coaster ride that we're told removes wastes and excess fluid from our bodies (but how do we really know? At least the old machines had a drip tube you could stick in a jug and measure, for God's sake!), while we wait to hit the jackpot on the Transplant Lottery… which simply means that in the midst of our rejoicing, another family grieves… and now we'll have to learn how to keep alive the death that lies inside us.

And so we cling to what you view as strange behavior for one simple reason: It's ours.

It's ours, and it's under our control. When Ms. Mary opens her bowl of salad, keep in mind that she mixed it herself, with no doctor or dietician looking over her shoulder, tut-tut-tutting about potassium levels or—horrors!!!—the dreaded Demon Phosphorus. She controls it, and no matter how much it reeks to high heaven and makes the particulate alarms go off, it's her small measure of comfort and a reminder of how she once prepared food for her family.

When Papa Joe plays Big Five on Three-Four and winks at himself, he's not cheating. (Well, he is, but that's not the point.) He plays dominoes and yells because that's what he did when he was young and strong and popular, and it's the one thing he has left that's truly his.

Well, as I conclude this essay, you may have been wondering what my oddity is. What hobby helps "improve my quality of life and helps me forget the many challenges kidney disease presents?"

When I walk in, I place my roller bag on my chair and begin to unpack. Snack, drink, headphones, and, finally, my HP laptop computer. I sit, and then the staff person assigned to me, like a spider approaching an unfortunate fly caught in its web, begins the task of connecting me to the hemodialysis machine for treatment. When she's done, I begin.

I'm a writer. I write prodigiously. I write with passion, as well as compassion. I write blogs, both political and humorous (well, at least I hope so!). I've written two books, and I'm working on a third. I write poetry, songs, and instructions on various aspects of life and living. I write because that sets me free from the chains that masquerade as tubes. And even if one day God blesses me, as I believe He will, and I'm set free from these sterile fetters, I shall continue to write, for my gift transcends my condition.

The Power of Water

Mary Wu

My father once told me, "The Chinese believe that the strongest substance in the world is water. Water appears innocent, but it's the only substance that can transform into another product, depending on its environment. When frozen, water turns into ice. When melted, water turns into liquid. Water has the power to destroy an entire population with tsunamis. Water has the power to turn into ice storms that can kill. We can't live without water. Water has a strength that no one could ever guess."

When I was a little girl, I was afraid of and fascinated by swimming and water. When I dipped my feet into the cool water for the first time and my curious reflection stared back at me, I knew I had to swim. My older sister was an avid swimmer who easily and gracefully flipped and turned in the water. I watched her enviously, wishing that I could swim, but my greatest wish was for a different life. All I had known since I was 3 years old was my chronic kidney failure, which revolved around dialysis, uncontrollable bladder issues, multiple procedures, hospitals, doctors, needles, nurses, and medicine. I was blessed to receive two kidney transplants, at age 6 and then at 12, but the health experiences never ended. I thought, "If only there were another world free from anything related to my health." That world was water.

I was 8 years old when I first tried to swim. I wore an inflatable lifesaver in the shape of a swan. My sister held my hand when I stepped into the water for the first time. The cold water numbed my body with excitement at what would happen next and made me forget anything health-related. My sister tried to teach me to kick and hold my breath. She took the lifesaver off me when I told her confidently that I could swim without it, but I started to sink. As much as I flailed my arms or tried to thrash my legs to kick, the power of the water and the chlorine attacked me. My sister grabbed me. I surfaced to catch my breath. My parents yelled at her, "Her legs aren't strong enough to kick or swim yet!"

Then, when I was either 10 or 11, I was invited to pool parties by a couple of my classmates. Those parties ended in disaster when I nearly drowned. My legs were still unexplainably weak, and I couldn't kick. I was frustrated: "How come everyone else can swim and kick and I can't?" Swimming and the water were these forces that I desired to face and overcome. If I could swim, I could turn anything that seemed impossible to possible.

When I was in my teens, I became close friends with a girl who was visually and hearing impaired. She was absolutely in love with swimming. Her impairments didn't stop her from plunging into the water from the diving board and doing front and back flips without goggles. I was mesmerized by her aquatic abilities. If she could swim, then so could I.

> When I'm in the water, I hear my father say how powerful water is, and I believe that *I* am water.

In the summers, she invited me to the swim club she belonged to so she could teach me how to swim. She taught me to lift my legs and kick in a fluid motion. We dunked our heads together under the water to hold our breath. She showed me how to slice my arms in and out of the water. Under the water was a whole other world of bubbles and blueness that I wanted to stay in forever. I understood why my friend and my sister loved swimming so much because water brought me to this magical place. The first time I swam a lap, kicking my legs and slicing my arms methodically, I squealed with joy and this overwhelming feeling of freedom filled me.

Swimming is still more than just a hobby to me, and I simply have to do it at least three or four times a week. Swimming keeps my mind, body, spirit, and soul balanced and clear. When I'm in the water, I forget about my health because I'm comforted, relaxed, and stronger than I could ever be and then empowered enough to overcome anything with my health when I'm outside of the water.

When I'm in the water, I hear my father say how powerful water is, and I believe that *I* am water.

2012 Essay Theme

What small act
of kindness by a
health care professional
made a difference
in your life?

The Case of the New Shoes

Sandra Kisselback

AFTER READING ABOUT THE THEME of this year's essay contest, I started thinking about all of the wonderful acts of kindness that have been bestowed on me by the many professionals in my corner while I've been living with kidney disease. One stellar act hit me like a lightning bolt. Remember this:

Brenda = the shining star... Shoes = smile, happy, fun, fun!

My journey with kidney disease began in 1992. From the very beginning, I've had a top-notch cast of health care providers to work with. One of the very first people I met was Brenda Cassidy, a social worker. My parents and I attended an informational meeting that told us what to expect as we entered the world of dialysis. Brenda was the speaker. After that meeting, my health challenges continued, but the only constant was my nephrologist.

Fast forward through peritoneal dialysis (1994), transplantation (1994-2006), peritoneal dialysis again (2006-2007), and finally home hemodialysis. I ran into Brenda Cassidy again in 2007, but the shoes didn't enter the picture until 2012, a full 20 years after I first met her.

So what about the shoes? My financial situation hasn't been the greatest since 2008. My shoes were old, ragged, and worn and were starting to come apart at the seams. Shoes weren't high on my list of things to spend money on. While it was embarrassing to go to the doctor and the clinic wearing this wretched pair of shoes, I just couldn't afford to buy another pair. Brenda apparently noticed.

While I was at the clinic for a routine matter, in she walked with a big smile on her face and an envelope in her hand. "We have an envelope for you with $50 in it. I noticed your shoes at our last office visit, and we wanted you to be able to dance in style." WOW!!!! Thank you, Brenda!

> Truthfully, whenever I wear those shoes, a newfound confidence comes over me.

I was dumbfounded at the generosity and compassion represented by this one small (but to me enormous) act of kindness. The tears flowed as I accepted this heartfelt gift coming from a special group of people who cared for me above and beyond my medical status. Wearing my new shoes to the next clinic visit put a bounce in my step.

Truthfully, whenever I wear those shoes, a newfound confidence comes over me. I'm no longer embarrassed by my footwear. Thank you to Brenda Cassidy, a health care professional and a true shining star who had a major role in the case of the new shoes... smile, happy, fun, fun!

Pillow Talk

Elizabeth Usher

HELLO. I DON'T USUALLY say anything, but I'd like to tell you a little bit about myself. I'm flexible, soft, and blue. I live in a cotton tote bag along with a rather nondescript blanket. My owner is on dialysis, and I was bought two years ago for a paltry sum, considering how special I am. My innards consist of movable wires, little beads like those found in Beanie Babies, and a soft exterior skin. And I'm telling you so much about myself because I figure prominently in a small act of kindness done by a... You get the picture.

My owner bought me because she sits in a Naugahyde recliner during dialysis, and the stiff attached pillow felt really uncomfortable against her neck. My wonderfully adjustable frame meant that she could wrap me around her neck and be comfortable, whether she was trying to watch TV at a strange angle or catch a little nap once in a while.

Then it happened.

I got a hole in my stitching: my little beads started popping out all over her and the floor of the dialysis center. She put me back into the tote and took me home. She wanted to sew up my wound, à la Dr. Oz, but, alas, her retinopathy makes it difficult for her to thread a needle. When her sister came over for a visit, my owner asked whether her sister would sew me up.

> I was bought two years ago
> for a paltry sum,
> considering how special I am.

The sister, a good-hearted soul actually, was too busy. She merely grabbed a wide strip of sticky mailing tape and covered the tear. I went back to dialysis with my owner, but after a few weeks my little beads started to escape again. And to make it worse, the tape had dried up and started to curl. Not only were my beads leaking out, but the tape was as scratchy as a tag on the neck of a cheap T-shirt!

My owner went back to the store where she got me to see whether she could find a clone, but to no avail. She went online to try to find another me, but I was the last of my kind.

Déjà vu. My owner again took me home, her sister again had no time to sew me up, and I again went back to the dialysis sessions with packing tape stuck over the tear. The beads still oozed out, the tape still curled and irritated my owner's neck, and now the tape started sticking to my owner's hair and pulling it out! She can't afford to lose any more hair. She was miserable. I was miserable.

Then it happened—that small act of kindness. As the technician was putting me into the tote, she looked very carefully at me and asked, "What's wrong with this pillow?"

"My sister tried to cover the hole," my owner said.

The technician looked at me again. She smiled at both of us and said, "I can fix this. I'll take it home, and it'll be as good as new."

And I was as good as new! The next dialysis day, I was sitting there waiting for my owner as she approached the chair. No more beads and no more sticky tape. I'd been operated on, and we both had a new lease on life.

My owner offered to pay the technician for sewing me up so beautifully, but she just smiled and said, "It wasn't that hard. I was glad to do it for you."

Thus, I was part of a professional's small act of kindness. My owner can now twist me to fit her neck, and there's no more tape to pull her hair out.

This small act of kindness in the form of a few stitches made a huge difference in both our lives.

Fist Bump

Keith Matthews

A FIST BUMP.

Defined by Merriam Webster as "a gesture in which two people bump their fists together (as in greeting or celebration)."

Fitting the definition of a "small act of kindness" perfectly, a fist bump, offered by my nephrologist, gave me my return ticket to humanity.

A little background is in order. Back in 2006, I was diagnosed with end-stage renal disease (ESRD), and, as a nurse, I understood the implications of this all too well. Ironically, I'd worked as a dialysis nurse for several years and assumed, as most nurses do, that I was intimately familiar with the physical and emotional trauma that patients with ESRD experience. After all, I mixed the dialysate bath, connected the water lines, injected the heparin into the tubes, and inserted the needles; I knew how it felt to be a dialysis patient!

Unfortunately, I found that life is much different when you're on the other side of the needle. I no longer had the luxury of deciding to take a day off and not go to the clinic or to schedule a much needed vacation. I now was on a schedule, a rude and uncaring taskmaster that demanded my presence at the appointed time and place for a prescribed 3½ hours, three times a week.

On one side of the needle, I was an important member of the health care team, one whose skills were sought after and valued. On the other side of the needle, however, I was demoted to the status of patient, who, regardless of what the bright and cheery posters in the waiting room claimed, was low man on the health care totem pole. All I had to look forward to now was being the recipient of glassy, frozen smiles and semi-intelligent questions asked in high-pitched, sing-song voices, "Are you taking your binders with every meal, Mr. Matthews?"

Sigh....

This particular treatment day started as they usually did, with chirpy aides buzzing around, putting patients on dialysis machines, and cooing gently to lessen the sting of #15 needles sliding into vascular access sites. Nurses, holding clipboards full of paper, waited their turn to ply their trade.

Doctors... ah! There he was, our resident Kidney the Kid, making what I would learn were his Friday morning rounds. I watched him closely, looking for some clue as to what I could expect from him. He was wearing jeans and a polo shirt: inconclusive, since nobody in here was expecting crisply starched scrubs. In fact, he could have walked in naked, and no one would have noticed. Well, almost no one—the lady in the corner was hastily putting on lipstick and eye liner. "Dang! I hope she doesn't poke herself in the eye," I thought.

"Miz Crawford, how do you feel?" he asked her.

"Ohhhh, Doctor," she breathed throatily, "I'm so... overloaded I just don't know what to do!"

> He was wearing jeans and a polo shirt: inconclusive, since nobody in here was expecting crisply starched scrubs.

I almost giggled; I hadn't seen a Mae West movie in years. "Uh-huh," he answered, looking at the nurse, who rolled her eyes. She was young; I made a mental note to tell her to keep practicing—she was getting really good at it.

"Well, Miz Crawford, let me adjust this machine to make sure it pulls all of your excess fluid, okay?"

"Well, not too much, Doctor," she pouted. "It took me a long time to get this fine!" She smoothed her hands over her hips; that took about 45 seconds or so. Miz Crawford had a lot of, er, fluid.

"Huh?" Doc looked momentarily confused, then the nurse tugged at his sleeve. "Come on, Doctor, new patient to see." He followed her like an obedient, well-trained greyhound.

"Well, well, what do we have... here?" Miz Crawford was still smoothing her hips; we both watched as she completed the operation. A cough made us turn our heads; the nurse eyed both of us sharply. "Your new patient, Doctor," she said, as she pointed to me. We looked at her, then at each other, a bit guiltily, I suppose.

"Nice to meet you, Mr. Matthews," he said, and offered his fist.

In that moment, we were no longer doctor and patient; we were just two men observing a woman bent on seduction. At that moment, all of the racial, cultural, educational, and professional barriers dropped away, and we made the briefest of contacts.

Fist bump.

This simple greeting, celebration of manhood, and small act of kindness made, and continues to make, a profound difference in my life.

A Doctor Who Cares

Donna Fink

IN THE 12 YEARS that I've been dealing with chronic renal failure, I've come to know many health care professionals. One in particular stands out, a nephrologist and the director of the dialysis center where I was being treated.

When I first met him, he wasn't my personal physician. I'd been experiencing severe back pain for several weeks; I started falling down and couldn't get up. I was 53 years old and certainly didn't expect to be having those kinds of physical problems. After mentioning my back pain to my doctor and others at the dialysis center, I was told that the facility was getting new chairs that should make my back feel better. I thought that something more than an uncomfortable chair was the problem, but I didn't know what else to do.

The director walked into the center one day just as I was leaving. I asked if I could have a moment of his time because I had a question and needed help. Even though I wasn't his patient, he took the time to listen to my concerns and took them seriously. He immediately called and arranged for a bone scan and an MRI. After I had the tests, he called to tell me that I had a staph infection that had settled in my spine. The infection, along with the effects of dialysis, had caused my spine to collapse, and it was pinching my spinal cord.

The fact that he stopped to listen to me that day literally saved my life. I spent four months on intravenous antibiotics before I underwent surgery. The surgeon discovered that thoracic vertebrae T4 through T9 had collapsed, and T6 and T7 had to be removed entirely and replaced with a cage. The remainder of my damaged spine was supported with rods. Within two weeks after I started rehabilitation, the wound got infected, and I had to face yet another surgery.

> The fact that he stopped to listen to me that day literally saved my life.

What I haven't said is that this doctor—the nephrologist and dialysis center director—followed my care as if I were his patient. After I had the second surgery, where they removed the necrotic tissue and resutured the incision, I couldn't walk. My husband was told to put me in a nursing home because I wouldn't get better and would probably die. He didn't listen and located a hospital that not only had an excellent rehabilitation facility, but could perform dialysis for me as well.

After months of rehabilitation, I was once again able to walk. I'm neither fast nor able to handle steps very well, but at least I'm vertical. If it hadn't been for the kindness shown to me by that doctor, I probably wouldn't be here.

I should mention another incident involving this same doctor. One day he was the attending physician at the hospital where I was a patient and had just paid me a visit. When he got ready to leave, I went to the door with him, intending to walk the corridors for my daily exercise. After he said goodbye, he slung his white coat over his shoulder and leisurely strolled past the nurses station, obviously ready to go home to his family. I noticed that he backed up a few steps and directed his attention to a patient who appeared to be in distress in a room a few doors down from mine. He stopped to ask a nurse whether she needed him to help. This person was also not his patient, but he took the time to ask whether his help was needed. You don't find many kind, compassionate, and caring physicians like him.

I told him the next time I saw him what I'd observed and that I'd never forget the kindness he'd shown to me and to others as well. He eventually did become my physician, and I'm so grateful to him for helping me when it seemed that no one else would.

I know that there are other health care professionals who are just as thoughtful and kind. To all of them, I'd like to say a very sincere thank you. It's because of people like them that lives have been saved or at least made better.

Crazy News

Heather Oman

Iᴛ's ᴄᴀʟʟᴇᴅ the doorknob question. You know, the doctor fin-
ishes examining a patient, stands up to end the visit, and, hand on
the doorknob, says, "Is there anything else?" The patient sees this as
her last opportunity to get more medical advice and tells the doctor
that even though she came in for a hangnail, she actually has had
chronic diarrhea for a month and pain in the joints and halitosis on
Tuesdays, and is there anything the doctor can do about this funny-
looking mole?

I'm told that doctors hate doorknob questions.

But I'll forever be grateful to the doctor who did the doorknob
act after he finished examining my sore throat. He opened the door
even before he paused and asked, "Is there anything else?" My sister
had been bugging me about my odd symptoms, telling me that I
needed to ask the doctor about the pain and numbness I was experiencing. I decided that this was my chance to get my sister off my
back. I cleared my throat.

"So, well, heh, it's kinda silly, but I've had numb toes for, you know, a while, and then sometimes my back and side hurt, and, ha ha, my sister said that I had to tell you because she says it's not normal, but I told her that it's nothing to worry about, right?"

> I'm told that doctors hate doorknob questions.

The doctor shut the door and said, "Wait. WHAT?"

I knew then that things might get serious.

He examined my toes, my legs, and my back; pricked my finger to test for diabetes; and moved my legs up and down, asking where it hurt. He took X-rays, made notes, and told me that he thought I might have a spinal tumor. He ordered an MRI, and I left his office, shell shocked. I'd gone in because I had a sore throat and now I was leaving to get an MRI!?

I was even more shocked when he called after the MRI to tell me that I had advanced polycystic kidney disease. The pain in my back was caused by my enlarged kidneys, and the numbness was due to pressure on my spinal nerves. But I liked the way he broke the news to me. He was calm and compassionate. At the end of the conversation, after we'd set up appointments and medication and taken that first step on the road to dealing with a chronic illness, he said, "Sorry about the crazy news. I know this wasn't what you expected."

He acknowledged that what he was telling me was crazy, surreal, impossible. It was this small act that made me laugh. I laughed again, feeling a little crazy myself. I said, "Exactly who expects to be diagnosed with polycystic kidney disease?" We laughed together. And his kindness and competence reassured me that, somehow, I'd figure all of this out.

It's been almost seven years since that phone call, and I've seen at least half a dozen more doctors. Some of them have had that same compassion, but I feel like nobody has treated me as well as the man who diagnosed me, who made me feel like my disease was crazy, but manageable. To be honest, I don't even remember his name. I doubt that he works in the same practice any more. For all I know, he could have moved to another city altogether.

But wherever he is, I'm sure that he's still treating patients with compassion, even as he acknowledges that the road they face will be hard.

And I'll bet that he still hates the doorknob question.

Ears to Hear

Susan Decuir

I MINDLESSLY FLIPPED THROUGH the well-worn magazines
in the waiting room until the nurse finally called my name. I
followed her down the hallway to the dreaded scales. She jotted
down my weight, then handed me a little plastic cup. Obediently,
I headed for the restroom. That annoying little job completed, I
entered the examination room, aka the freezer, where the nurse
checked my blood pressure, then inserted a needle into my most
cooperative vein. "Leave me enough to live on," I always teased as
I watched my blood drain into the little vials. She giggled as usual
and left the room.

Checking my watch every few minutes, I prayed that I
wouldn't be late for work when in walked a pleasant woman wearing a fashionably long skirt and a colorful blouse. She extended
her hand, smiled, and looked directly into my eyes. "Hi, I'm Dr.
Peri. I'm sorry, but your regular doctor won't be in today."

I liked her immediately. She was professional, personable,

and a great listener—the opposite of my regular doctor. His bedside manner was insensitive at best: like the time he told me that people with hereditary polycystic kidney disease shouldn't have children (I had two). He obviously doesn't know or believe that children are a gift from God, I thought, and didn't mind telling him so.

Dr. Peri treated me like a real person with a heart, a mind, and a spirit, not a mere entry on her daily calendar. I learned more about my disease from her that day than I'd gotten from the doctor I'd been seeing for years. I felt that she truly cared about helping me get better. And when I asked questions, she answered them, because she actually listened.

"Dr. Peri, I have one more question before I leave," I said, pushing myself off the chair.

She lifted her dark, caring eyes from her paperwork, looked at me, and listened.

"Would it be okay if I changed doctors and saw you from now on?"

"Certainly, if that's what you want to do," she said and smiled sweetly.

And I did.

When Dr. Peri suggested that I begin taking shots to counter the anemia and boost the waning energy caused by my kidney disease, I said that I would first like to pray about it with my husband, Ron. Though her faith differed from ours, she honored my request and never pressured. She just—well—listened, but made sure that I understood the benefits of taking the shots and the risks of not taking them.

I listened to my doctor and to God and began the biweekly shots. My energy level improved, and I was able to keep up with my energetic, curious, adorable first grandbaby, a little boy named Evan.

In 2008, Dr. Peri advised that it was time to begin the screening process necessary to get approved for a transplant. "My husband and I will pray about it," I said, standing in faith and believing that God had a miracle for me. I knew Dr. Peri thought it urgent that I begin the process immediately, but she remained patient with me and honored my faith. I appreciated that.

> Dr. Peri treated me like a real person with a heart, a mind, and a spirit, not a mere entry on her daily calendar.

A year passed, and my kidney function dropped to 8%. Ron and I knew that it was time to put action to our faith. Dr. Peri quickly got the paperwork in motion, never reprimanding me for having waited so long. She just—you know—listened.

Having passed the health screening, I was approved for the transplant list on April 17, 2009. Following two surgeries on my left arm to prepare a fistula for dialysis, with a third yet to be scheduled, I received a phone call from Methodist Transplant saying that they had a perfect match for me, two months and ten days after I was put on the list. Ron and I thanked God all the way to the hospital for the miracle my family and friends had prayed for.

I went home four days after surgery. Three years have passed without any complications. I thank God for my health and for the abundance of energy I'll have for rocking and cuddling my third grandbaby, due in November.

Thank you, Dr. Peri, for listening, and thank you, God, for hearing our prayers and for bringing my miracle in your own time, which is always perfect. And thank you to the man who listened with his heart when he signed a donor card. "He who has ears to hear—let him hear." (Matthew 11:15)

2012 Honorable Mention

Have My Cake and Eat It Too

Katie Holland

SOMETHING QUITE MAGICAL HAPPENS when I eat a slice of cake. Once a bite of cake hits my mouth, all of a sudden my problems are solved and the world is at peace, as long as the icing is coating my tongue and the cake slides down my throat. It's a moment of pleasure and a time to celebrate. You might think that as a dialysis patient, I'd have less to celebrate and fewer reasons to eat cake, and if it weren't for Rosetta, my patient care technician, I might think so too.

Having been on dialysis for a year, I knew the rules. No food is allowed in the area where we dialyze. To be honest, I didn't worry much when they took down the sign during a recent remodeling. After all, four hours is a long time, and I see nothing wrong with eating a snack. Obviously, I didn't think that anyone, particularly one of the paid employees, would dare risk his or her job to break a rule. No way!

Yet one Saturday, it hit me. I'd been on dialysis for a whole year. I'd endured three sessions a week for an entire year—52 weeks of needle sticks, blood pressure drops, and really bad cramps. I couldn't possibly see a reason to celebrate. I jokingly asked my nurse and my technicians, "Hey, do we serve cake on a patient's anniversary?" Knowing that this would be against the rules, I assumed that they gathered from my tone that I was being flippant and would go on with their work.

Well, as soon as I mentioned this, Rosetta started plotting a prohibited cake delivery. She waited until her short lunch break to find exactly what she felt was the perfect concoction of butter, sugar, and flour worthy of anyone's craving, and once she arrived back at work, she found me and placed an aluminum-wrapped package in my lap.

> With that first taste, the euphoria of eating cake struck me.

Surprised by her gift, I wasn't exactly sure what to think. Did this woman really break a rule just for me? Why would she risk it? She could have gotten into trouble for this! After a few minutes, I opened the package. There it was, a slice of lemon pound cake with a light glaze on top. Oh, this was serious! I just knew that this was intended for after my session. That's what my brain kept telling me, but my taste buds screamed with bliss, and I had to take a bite of this perfect creation.

With that first taste, the euphoria of eating cake struck me. It tasted just like the cupcakes I'd had in elementary school. As a result, I wanted to hold onto each flavor profile that hit my tongue: sweet, sour, and savory. I literally had a slice of heaven in my lap. It tasted oh, so perfect.

Now with this goodness having left my mouth and made its way to my stomach, it was as if all of my problems had disappeared. No longer was I sitting hooked up to a dialysis machine, I was transported to some joyous times like my college graduation and Christmas Day. I began to reflect on what I should already have been remembering on my 1-year anniversary: I thought of all of the times I swam in my parents' pool this summer and the fun I'd had with my family and friends. I thought about all of the George Clooney movies I saw this year and how much I love them. I also reflected on the visit to my aunt and uncle's home in Arizona. This was the first time I'd seen where they live. None of those things would have been possible without my going to dialysis three times a week for this entire year.

As my session ended, I didn't get a chance to thank Rosetta. She was too busy getting her work done for the day, but I'll forever be grateful for that simple gift. It took only a little lemony glaze to remind me of the life that I have to be thankful for!

My Guardian Angel

Kristi Flynn

IT'S BEEN SAID THAT "doctors diagnose, but nurses cure." In dealing with chronic kidney disease (CKD), I've found this to be true, especially in my dialysis clinic in Augusta, Georgia. I'm blessed to be in the care of several amazing nurses, and I could readily write an essay about each and every one of them, but this story is about Miss Becca—my first nurse. She's the one who pulled me through my darkest times and helped me become the well-educated, self-advocating patient I am today.

When I first started peritoneal dialysis in 2009, I was scared, confused, overwhelmed, and—most notably—very ill. You could see it in my pale skin, hear it in my tired voice, and, of course, observe it in my impressively awful lab results. I needed help! When I met Miss Becca, she made it clear that she was going to do whatever it took to get me better. I would soon find out that this included everything from replying to my frantic text messages in the middle of the night to popping in for unscheduled home visits just to check on me. She never wanted anything in return except for me to feel better.

That was reward enough for her. I could see that she was fighting for me every day, and I always knew that she had my best interests at heart. Until I was strong enough to advocate for myself, she was my advocate. She never let me get discouraged and always pushed me to make dialysis work for me, even if that meant stepping outside of what was considered the norm. She knew that each patient was an individual and that what worked for one person didn't necessarily work for another.

> I could see that she was fighting for me every day, and I always knew that she had my best interests at heart.

The best advice I ever received came from Miss Becca, and I still carry it with me in my heart as I continue to live with CKD. She said, "You're special. No one can know exactly how you're feeling or what you're experiencing except you, and you're your own best advocate." Those words and that sentiment have helped me live a relatively healthy, normal life on dialysis for the past three years.

Miss Becca gave me the knowledge and the power I needed to take control of my treatment, to know my disease better than anyone else, and thus to be a model patient. I might ask a lot of questions, but no one will ever accuse me of being uninformed! I believe that the reason I've never developed any major problems or required any hospital stays is because of the valuable lessons I learned in those first few weeks of training.

I consider Miss Becca to be a guardian angel who was sent to me during the worst time in my life to help me become the well-adjusted patient I am today. And even though she's no longer my nurse, she's made it clear that I can call her whenever I need advice or an encouraging word. She still keeps tabs on me in a way that only the best nurses can, with questions like, "Are you taking your medicine, Kristi?" or "Is that dinner you're eating low in phosphorus, Kristi?"

And I say, "Yes, Miss Becca, of course! You taught me well." I only wish that every dialysis patient could have such an amazing nurse, advocate, and friend. It would make CKD's long, trying road so much easier.

Words that Changed My Life

Shari Gilford

I sat with my parents in the waiting room, perspiring from anxiety. This transplant team would decide my future. Would they accept me? I thought about everything that had led up to this nerve-wracking moment.

In May 1987 I graduated from college. The 99%-matched kidney that my older brother had donated to me ten years earlier had been working perfectly, allowing me to live my dreams. I forgot that I had kidney disease. I also forgot to take my medication. When nothing bad happened, I figured that I didn't need it anymore.

A year after graduation, I caught a cold that lingered and got worse. I was feverish off and on, and I even lost my appetite for my favorite foods. My recent lab results had been normal, so I didn't suspect that my kidney might be failing.

My mother finally convinced me to make an appointment with my nephrologist. This man cared for me like a daughter—I was his only young patient and the same age as his son.

I waited nervously for him to reveal the test results. He looked directly at me from across his large desk as he spoke each word deliberately: "If you had waited another week to see me, you wouldn't be sitting here."

He paused to let this sink in. Turning to my parents, he explained, "The only way her kidney could fail so quickly is either because of a trauma to the kidney or because she stopped taking her medication."

Cheerfulness had been my hallmark,
but now guilt, self-condemnation, remorse,
and a deep sense of loss overwhelmed me.

I felt numb. The words were like daggers thrown at my guilty conscience. What I had been hiding for over a year was starkly exposed. My doctor knew what I had done.

He finished with clinical detachment. He would place an emergency catheter in my neck the following day and I would begin dialysis—an abrupt end to my carefree youth.

The next few months were among the most difficult in my life. The relationship with my doctor seemed irreparably broken. One of the nurses who had worked with him for years told me that she had never seen him so upset. Could I ever regain his trust?

I had caused my parents grief and disappointment, even though they quickly forgave me. My brother was upset because I hadn't taken care of his gift to me. Cheerfulness had been my hallmark, but now guilt, self-condemnation, remorse, and a deep sense of loss overwhelmed me.

After a few difficult months on hemodialysis, I decided to switch to peritoneal dialysis (PD). I hoped PD would help me prove I was trustworthy. I would have to do it consistently several times a day. Maybe I could rebuild my doctor's trust in me.

After a year without mishaps, my PD nurse, Cindy, encouraged me to get another transplant. However, the transplant surgeon decided that I was a high-risk candidate due to my history of "medication non-compliance." He refused to accept me for a transplant.

I was devastated. In an instant his words had yanked hope out of my heart.

Now what? Dialysis forever? I was only 25 years old and had my whole life ahead of me. I longed to be free again.

Cindy listened compassionately as disappointment overflowed from the depths of my soul.

"This is *your* life," she replied gently, yet with authority. "Do you want a transplant? Then you can get one. Make appointments with every transplant center you can find. Treat it like a job interview. Be honest about your history, but be confident. This is for you. Go after it and don't give up. I support you." Her confidence in me filled my heart with hope again.

Now I was sitting in the waiting room at the transplant center, wondering whether this was the day that would set my life on a new path. I'd seen a succession of nurses, doctors, and social workers, and now it was time for the surgeon to weigh the evidence and pronounce the verdict. I'd heard he was a tough man who spoke bluntly and had little tolerance for someone who didn't take care of her kidney.

This man would decide my fate.

On Mother's Day, 1990, the call came. The tough surgeon had given me a second chance. He also became a good friend.

Cindy, my cheerleader and PD nurse, gave me the courage to keep believing, and I'm deeply grateful. Her words changed my life.